Manchester United

THEN AND NOW

First published in the United Kingdom in 2011 by
Batsford
Old Magistrate's Court
10 Southcombe Street
London
W14 0RA

An imprint of Anova Books Company Ltd
Copyright © Anova Books 2011

The moral rights of the author have been asserted

ISBN: 978-1-84994-033-7

A CIP catalogue record for this book is available from the British Library.

16 15 14 13 12 11 10 9 8 7 6 5 4 3 2 1

Reproduction by Rival Colour Ltd, UK
Printed by 1010 Printing International Ltd, China

This book can be ordered direct from the publisher at the website: www.anovabooks.com

The author would like to thank Ian Welch, Graham Betts, Drew Heatley and Mike Gent for their help with specialist knowledge.

PHOTO CREDITS
The publisher wishes to thank the following for kindly providing photographs for this book:

Getty Images: Pages 4, 8,10,12,14, 18, 19, 20, 27, 28, 29a, 30, 31, 32, 34, 35, 36, 37b, 38, 40, 41a, 42a, 44b, 47a, 47b, 48a, 48b, 49a, 52a, 52b, 53a, 53b, 55a, 55c, 56, 57, 58b, 59, 67c, 70, 71a, 71b, 72a, 73b, 73c, 74a, 75a, 76a, 78a, 79a, 79b, 80a, 81b, 81c, 83a, 90b, 92, 93b, 94a, 94b, 95b, 100a, 101a,101b, 103c, 105c, 106c, 107, 108b,111a, 112b, 113a, 113b, 117, 124, 127a, 130, 138, 139b.

Mirrorpix: Pages 9, 16, 17, 26, 29b, 44a, 46, 49b, 50a, 62b, 65a, 66, 67a, 68, 69a, 72b, 73a, 75b, 75c, 78b, 81a, 83b, 84a, 84b, 87a, 89a, 89b, 91a, 93a, 95a, 96a, 97a, 99a, 100b, 102a, 103a, 103b, 104a, 106a, 108a, 109a, 110, 114, 115, 122, 123a, 125, 128, 131, 132, 133a, 134, 135a, 136, 137, 140.

Aidan O'Rourke: Pages 7b, 11, 13, 15, 21, 31b, 33b, 43, 47c, 51, 55b, 61a, 61c, 63, 65b, 67b, 84c, 87c, 89c, 91b, 97c, 99b, 109b, 111b, 119, 121, 123b, 127b, 129, 143.

Manchester Archives and Local Studies at Manchester Central Library: Pages 20b, 22, 23, 33a, 60, 61b, 62a, 90a, 98, 112a, 120, 126.

Corbis Images: Pages 6, 7, 50b, 77, 79a, 82, 83c, 133b, 135b, 142.

Rex Features: Pages 37a, 39a, 58a, 64, 69b, 97b, 105a, 105b.

TopFoto: Pages 54, 86, 87b, 118.

Press Association/PA Images: Pages 42b, 88, 116, 141.

Neil Langford: Page 45b.

About the author

Michael Heatley is the former editor of *The Footballer* and *Matchday* magazines. He has also written for a number of national publications including *4-4-2* and the *Radio Times*. He is the author of *Football Grounds Then and Now, A History of Football, Football Club Origins and Nicknames, Lost Football League Grounds* and *The Football Grounds Factbook*. He has interviewed many players and managers over the years including United legends George Best and Edwin van der Sar.

Cover photos (clockwise from top left): Old Trafford viewed from above in 1966 (Getty Images); Rio Ferdinand and Ryan Giggs hold the Champions League trophy aloft in 2008 (Getty Images); Old Trafford from above in 2006 (Getty Images); United's European Cup squad pose with the 1968 trophy at the start of the 1968-69 season (Getty Images).

Back cover photo: United players celebrate their League Championship win with manager Matt Busby on the pitch at Old Trafford following their draw with Stoke City in May 1967 (Mirrorpix).

Photo below: Warwick Road on match day 1960 (Manchester Archives and Local Studies at Manchester Central Library).

Manchester United

THEN AND NOW

Michael Heatley

BATSFORD

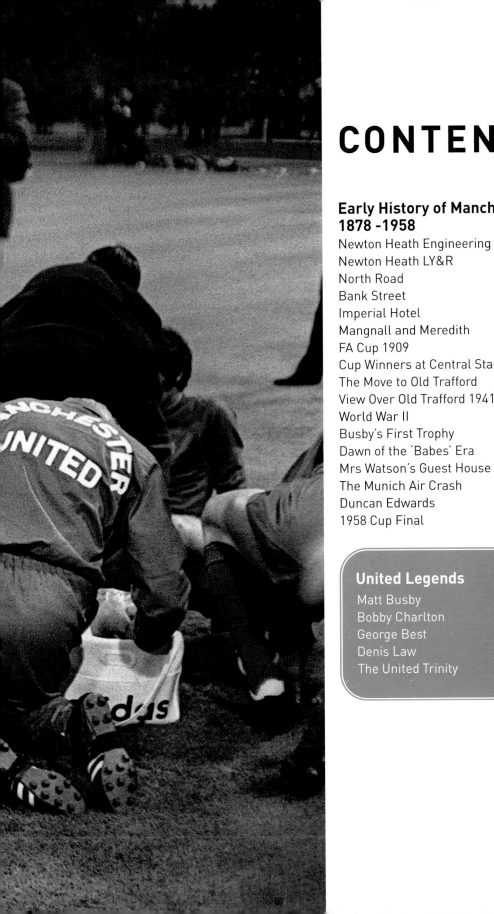

CONTENTS

Early History of Manchester United FC 1878 -1958

Newton Heath Engineering Works	6
Newton Heath LY&R	8
North Road	10
Bank Street	12
Imperial Hotel	14
Mangnall and Meredith	16
FA Cup 1909	18
Cup Winners at Central Station	20
The Move to Old Trafford	22
View Over Old Trafford 1941	24
World War II	26
Busby's First Trophy	28
Dawn of the 'Babes' Era	30
Mrs Watson's Guest House	32
The Munich Air Crash	34
Duncan Edwards	44
1958 Cup Final	46

United Legends

Matt Busby	48
Bobby Charlton	70
George Best	80
Denis Law	92
The United Trinity	96

Life at MUFC

Travel by Plane	56
Travel by Rail	58
Getting to the Game	60
Away from the Pitch	64
The Midland Hotel	66
WAGS and Glamour	68
Supporter Power	76
Autograph Hunters	78
Any Other Business?	90
United Stars and Their Cars	98
Training Regimes	106
The Cliff	108
Trafford Training Centre, Carrington	112

Trophies

FA Cup 1963	114
European Cup 1968	116
Albert Square 1968	118

Old Trafford Stadium

Warwick Road on Match Day	120
Red Devils Shop	122
From Pre-War to Post-War	124
Dawn of the Sixties	126
Stadium Rebuilding	128
The Tunnel	132
Fencing the Stretford End	134
Post Hillsborough	136
Into the 21st Century	138
Pilgrimages	140
Lights on at the Theatre of Dreams	142

NEWTON HEATH ENGINEERING WORKS

'THE RAILWAY MEN'

The football club which evolved into Manchester United was founded in 1878 by workers at the Carriage and Wagon Department at Lancashire and Yorkshire Railway's Newton Heath depot in north-east Manchester. The team was dubbed Newton Heath L&YR to distinguish it from Motive Power division side Newton Heath Loco.

The railway connection was strong. The company funded the club and paid the rent on their ground, North Road, which was situated close to the depot, although the changing rooms were half a mile away at the Three Crowns pub on Oldham Road. The Dining Room Committee of the Carriage and Wagon Department administered team affairs. The Heathens' half-gold, half-green shirts were based on the company's livery.

Newton Heath's initial matches were friendlies against sides from other Lancashire and Yorkshire Railway divisions in addition to those from other railway undertakings. As the team's prowess increased, they sought more testing opponents. In 1883-84 Newton Heath had their first competitive match, which they lost 7-2 to Blackburn Olympic in the Lancashire Cup. In 1886-87, the club's first FA Cup tie ended in disarray when they refused to play extra time after a 2-2 draw at Fleetwood. Their opponents were subsequently awarded the match and Newton Heath boycotted next season's competition in protest.

In the photo above, a railway carriage emerges from the Newton Heath works in March 1927. Carriages and wagons were built here until it closed in 1932, despite the works having one of the largest rolling stock outputs in Britain.

▲ LANCASHIRE AND YORKSHIRE RAILWAY

Formerly a farming area, Newton Heath is a name taken from Old English meaning the 'new town on the heath'. The heath after which the locality was named formerly stretched from Miles Platting to Failsworth. The area rapidly transformed during the 19th century with engineering becoming the principal industry, although mining and textile factories were also big employers in the area.

Newton Heath Carriage and Wagon works opened in 1877, producing and repairing carriages and wagons for the Lancashire & Yorkshire Railway. The LYR was incorporated in 1847 from an amalgamation of several existing railways and provided vital employment following the Industrial Revolution.

The works used motor vehicles (above) to transport equipment and parts around the site and to collect and deliver parts.

▶ TODAY

By the time of the works' closure, the LYR had already amalgamated with the London and North Western Railway (LNWR) in January of 1922. Today, the site has been redeveloped into Central Park, formerly the North Manchester Business Park. The large, cable-stayed canopy shown here shelters a twin-track Metrolink tram station sited on a newly constructed bridge.

NEWTON HEATH L&YR

THE HEATHENS

In 1895, Newton Heath L&YR reached the first Finals of the Manchester and District Senior Cup. Beaten finalists then, they returned in 1886 to claim the club's first trophy and achieved a hat-trick of wins in the competition from 1888 to 1890.

The Lancashire and Yorkshire Railway backed the team's success by offering jobs to well-known players like Roger and Jack Doughty and Jack Powell so that they could turn out for Newton Heath.

The Heathens' first taste of league football was in the 20-team Combination, a rival to the Football League that began in the same year, 1888. Financial and organisational problems led to the Combination folding before its fixtures were completed.

In 1890, after their application for league membership gained only one vote, Newton Heath joined 11 other clubs to form the Football Alliance. Two years later, the league expanded to two divisions by merging with the Alliance. Second place in the final Alliance table entitled the Heathens to be elected directly to the First Division. Finishing bottom in their first season, they escaped the drop by winning a 'Test Match' against Division Two champions Small Heath. Next season, after another last-place finish, they lost the Test Match to Liverpool and were relegated.

Pictured here, the 1888-89 season was also their first in the Football Alliance. Players in this auspicious team line-up (above left) include, back row: Mitchell, Slater, McMillan; middle row: Roger Doughty, Ramsey, Owen; front row: Smith (umpire), Farman, Jack Doughty, Evans, Malarvie, Sharp, Preddy (trainer).

SAM BLACK

Sam Black (pictured above in 1885) has been labelled the first star of Newton Heath and so set the benchmark for all those who followed. A no-nonsense full back, Black – club captain between 1883 and 1887 – was selected with three of his team-mates to play for the Manchester and District FA representative team against their Liverpudlian counterparts in March 1884. It was common for district and international players to wear the badge of their local association or home country on their club shirts during this era and Black's badge can clearly be seen on the left hand side. He later went on to become a referee and, on one occasion, reportedly disallowed an Arsenal goal because the ball burst on its way to the net and the keeper couldn't thus stop it due to its skewed trajectory.

THE GHOSTS OF NEWTON HEATH

Little did the team realise back in 1993, when (from left to right) Lee Sharpe, Mark Hughes, Alex Ferguson, Paul Parker and Eric Cantona dressed up in replica kit and moustaches, that the team's strip and colours would become a symbol of resistance to a future ownership.

United played a number of matches with the green and gold replica third kit during the 1992-93 season, the Premier League's inaugural campaign, and retained it for the following year. The retro-style lace-up collar also appeared on home shirts, while regular away shirts changed from round-necked and blue (1992-93) to black and gold (1993-95). It's a classic kit that, to this day, remains one of the most loved by the fans. By the next time United fans picked up the green and gold scarves in 2009, Eric Cantona had developed a film acting career that stretched over 10 years including the enigmatic biopic, *Looking For Eric*.

CANTONA'S ENIGMATIC CAREER

Eric Daniel Pierre Cantona (far right) played for Auxerre, Martigues, Marseille, Bordeaux, Montpellier, Nîmes and Leeds United before finishing his career at Manchester United. He made just 144 appearances for the club but won four Premier League titles in five years as well as two FA Cups. In 1995 the enigmatic Frenchman was suspended from the game for eight months after a Kung Fu attack on a Crystal Palace supporter who had been shouting abuse at him as he left the pitch. At a press conference afterwards he gave what would become the classic Eric Cantona quote: 'When the seagulls follow the trawler, it's because they think sardines will be thrown into the sea,' and left. His United high point was the 1996 FA Cup Final where he captained the side and scored the winning goal in a 1-0 win over Liverpool. After indulging in a part-time acting career, he became Director of Soccer at the New York Cosmos in January 2011.

NORTH ROAD

▶ TEAM OF 1892

The Newton Heath team of 1892, the year they joined the Football League. Bob Donaldson (front row centre, with the ball) scored the club's first league goal in their first ever league match, a game that ended in a 4-3 defeat at Blackburn Rovers. The centre-forward, who had previously played for Airdrieonians and Blackburn Rovers, went on to score 66 times in 155 appearances before retiring in 1897.

TROUBLE AT NORTH ROAD

Newton Heath's attempts to join the Football League were hampered by the shortcomings of their North Road ground, particularly its muddy, gravel-strewn playing surface which often caused visiting teams to complain. By 1885, when football first turned professional, the pitch had been enclosed and supporters were charged admission to help pay the players' wages. To secure league status, the club needed to increase the capacity from 12,000 and, in 1891, two grandstands capable of holding 1,000 spectators each were purchased.

This put the club at odds with the Lancashire and Yorkshire Railway who refused to contribute to the cost of the stands and stopped paying the rent on North Road. Although most of the players remained railway employees, the suffix 'L&YR' was dropped in 1892 and the club became a separate entity. The site's owners, the Manchester Cathedral authorities, objected to the admission charges and served Newton Heath with an eviction notice in June 1893.

The search for another ground, which had begun in 1891, was intensified and an existing sports stadium three miles away in Bank Street, Clayton (see page 12), became Newton Heath's new home at the start of 1893-1894, their second league season. The two grandstands could, sadly, not be accommodated and were sold at the knockdown price of £100 each.

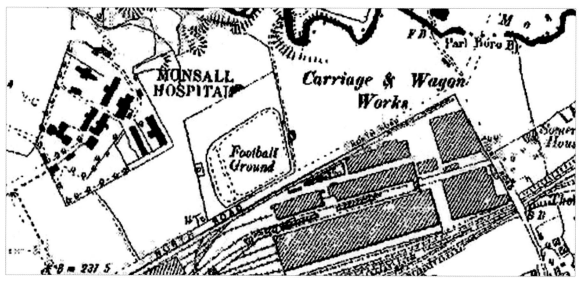

TODAY

Although the North Road ground no longer exists and even the road itself has been renamed Northampton Road, it did provide a recreational area for local residents after the departure of Newton Heath in 1893. The site was eventually developed into Moston Brook High School and, for a while, a red plaque explaining its heritage was proudly displayed on one of the building's walls until it was stolen. The school closed in 2000 and the area was subsequently chosen to be the North Manchester Business Park with the former site of the ground currently occupied by the offices of Japanese multinational computer hardware and IT services company Fujitsu.

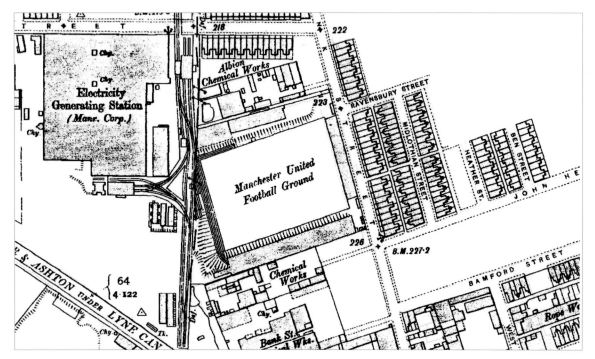

BANK STREET

PITCH BATTLE

Bank Street was a stronghold for Newton Heath in 1894-95 as they went undefeated at home in their quest to return to the top flight at the first attempt, having been relegated in 1893-94. Third place was enough to earn them a Test Match against First Division Stoke City which they lost 3-0. Unfortunately, the pitch was little improvement on their previous home and suffered from waterlogging so often that sand had to be laid over the surface.

The problematic Bank Street pitch was not the only matter for concern. Life in the Second Division was proving difficult and the club's increasingly precarious finances were worsened by an ill-advised court case against the *Birmingham Gazette* which alleged that the team were using strong arm tactics to win games. The judge awarded Newton Heath a farthing in damages and ordered both parties to pay their own costs.

After another unsuccessful Test Match followed in 1897, winning the Lancashire Senior Cup in 1898 proved little respite. Subsequent seasons saw attendances decline and debts mount as the club was unable to find its way out of Division Two, slipping to fifteenth position in 1901-02, its last season as Newton Heath.

Pictured above are the Newton Heath team that defeated Walsall Town Swifts by a 14-0 scoreline in a Division Two match in March 1895. This record victory did not stand, however, as Walsall successfully appealed against the result because of the state of the Bank Street pitch. Newton Heath won the re-match 9-0 in April. Back row, left to right: Albut (Secretary), Paley (trainer), Dow, Douglas, Palmer (Director), Errentz, Davidson, Faulkner (Director). Middle row: Crompton (President), Perrins, McNaught, Stewart, Jones (Vice-President). Front row: Clarkin, Donaldson, Cassidy, Smith and Peters.

TODAY

Despite eventually boasting a capacity of around 50,000, the stadium was not equal to the ambitions of the club and they moved out in 1910. Renovations and repairs had been somewhat neglected towards the end of the club's residency at Bank Street with all eyes on their new home so it was no surprise to locals when the main stand blew down in a storm shortly after the club left.

The Bank Street site had various industrial uses for the remainder of the 20th century until it was cleared as part of the construction of the Manchester Velodrome in the early Nineties. The exact site of the former stadium is now concealed from view under the tarmac of the Manchester Velodrome car park (above), although a red plaque adorns one of the houses opposite to indicate its importance in United's history.

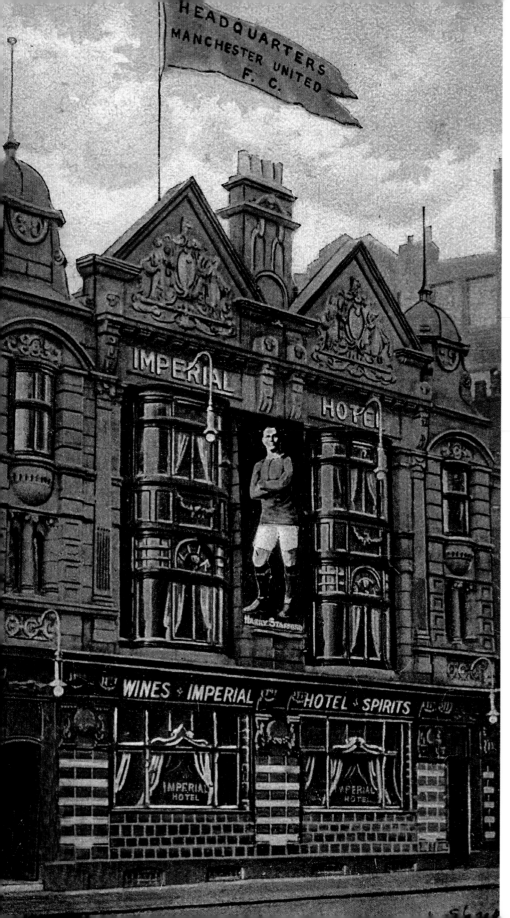

THE IMPERIAL HOTEL

◄ MANCHESTER UNITED HQ

The Imperial Hotel in Manchester had a notable place in early football history. Not only was it the 'headquarters of Manchester United' after the club changed its name from Newton Heath in 1902, it was also a favoured venue of the Players' Union (now the Professional Footballers' Association) with the inaugural meeting taking place here in December 1907. This Edwardian postcard, bearing the image of United club captain Harry Stafford, clearly displays the link between the hotel and club while another United stalwart, Charlie Roberts, was one of the driving forces behind the Players' Union. Stafford later became licensee of the hotel following his retirement in 1903.

J.H. DAVIES TURNS HEATH INTO UNITED

John Henry Davies was a self-made man with an eye for investment to whom Harry Stafford turned in 1901. Stafford attempted to persuade the wealthy brewer to invest in the club but, as legend has it, it took the intervention of his dog for his dreams to succeed. Needing to find at least £1,000 to survive, a four-day bazaar was held to raise funds for Newton Heath. It soon became clear that this would not be enough. On the final day a St Bernard dog with a collection box strapped to its back escaped and found its way to the home of the local brewing tycoon. Davies' daughter Elsie was so enthralled with the animal that its owner agreed to let her keep it ... if her father took over the club. Davies organised a consortium of four businessmen who each contributed £500 to rescue Newton Heath.

Meanwhile, Heathens' president William Healey had applied for a winding-up order because of the money he was owed. The club hovered on the brink until the Football League approved the takeover plan. John Henry Davies, soon installed as Chairman, was instrumental in changing the club's name to Manchester United, a suggestion of groundsman and future chief scout Louis Rocca. At the same time, the club's colours were standardised to the famous red and white.

Davies' wealth would help transform the club into a major force in English football.

TODAY

The site of the former Imperial Hotel, which was later rechristened the Mancunian, is now the Malmaison Hotel. The inset photo shows the building as it looked in 1986 before its demolition, although by that time it had lost most of its associations with the club. The Malmaison has a suite christened 'The Best' decked out in red and black and dedicated to George Best, whose own Slack Alice nightclub in Bloom Street wouldn't have been too far to walk to, had it continued in business.

MANGNALL AND MEREDITH

◄ PROMOTION AT THE THIRD ATTEMPT

Ernest Mangnall was appointed as United manager – or 'secretary', as the position was then known – a few games into the 1903-04 season, having previously been a director at Bolton Wanderers and secretary at Burnley. Funded by Chairman J.H. Davies, he guided the club to promotion at the third attempt in 1905-06. Two years later, United won the First Division Championship and 1908-09 saw them lift the inaugural Charity Shield together with their first FA Cup. Another league title followed in 1911 and his final trophy was the Charity Shield before leaving United for Manchester City in 1912.

One of Mangnall's most important signings was Welsh winger Billy Meredith. Often described as football's first superstar, Meredith arrived at United with three other ex-Manchester City stars, Sandy Turnbull, Jimmy Bannister and Herbert Burgess, after City were found guilty by the FA of making illegal payments and forced to sell their players at auction. In addition to helping United win its first major trophies, Meredith, along with Charlie Roberts, set up the original professional footballers' union. He returned to City in 1921 and played on, with trademark toothpick in mouth, until the age of 49.

This photograph shows the Manchester United players who clinched promotion from the Second Division in 1905-06. Back row, left to right: Alec Downie, Harry Moger, Bob Bonthron. Middle row, left to right: Ernest Mangnall (Secretary), Jack Picken, Charles Sagar, Tommy Blackstock, Jack Peddie, Fred Bacon (Trainer). Front row, left to right: John Beddow, Charlie Roberts, Alec Bell, Tommy Arkesden.

► BILLY MEREDITH

Billy Meredith won League Championship winning medals with United in 1908 and 1911 as well as the 1909 FA Cup. The Welshman had been accused of match-fixing allegations during his time with rivals Manchester City and joined the red half of Manchester during his subsequent ban. He went on to play more than 300 games for United in a career spanning 15 years before heading back to City to see out his playing days.

► FA CHARITY SHIELD

Having clinched their first Division One title, United took on Southern League champions Queens Park Rangers in the inaugural FA Charity Shield match on 27 April 1908. The game ended in a 1-1 draw, with Billy Meredith scoring his side's goal at Stamford Bridge. Following a four-month gap, the tie was replayed – again at Stamford Bridge – with United this time running out 4-0 victors courtesy of a Jimmy Turnbull hat-trick and a strike from George Wall.

CHARLIE ROBERTS/FA CUP 1909

▲ INSPIRATIONAL CAPTAIN

Grimsby Town centre-half Charlie Roberts was one of manager Ernest Mangnall's first signings for United for a record fee of £400. Strong, quick and talented, he was the lynchpin of a tight defensive unit that helped United gain automatic promotion in 1906 and then secure league and cup triumphs. Something of a rebel, Darlington-born Roberts co-founded the first players' union with Billy Meredith and was censured by the FA for breaking their rules by wearing shorts above the knee.

Appointed captain in 1905-06, Roberts helped convince Mangnall that Sandy Turnbull should play in the 1909 Cup Final, despite a niggling knee injury. Turnbull scored the only goal of the Final at Crystal Palace against Bristol City. United went down to 10 men when left-back Vince Hayes was injured; substitutes were not allowed in those days. Hayes returned as a forward as United fought a successful rearguard action to emerge victorious.

Roberts was the first United captain to lift the FA Cup and the League Championship trophy. He became the club's first England international, winning three caps. He was transferred to Oldham Athletic in 1913 for £1,500 – another record.

United's 1909 FA Cup winning squad is shown above. Top row (from left to right): Alex Downie, Herbert Burgess. Second row: J. Taylor (Director), J. Nuttall (Assistant Trainer), Harry Stafford (Director), Herbert Broomfield, George Stacey,

Dick Duckworth, Dick Holden, Alex Bell, Harry Moger, Fred Bacon (Trainer), Ernest Mangnall (Manager). Seated: Jack Picken, Jimmy Bannister, Jimmy Turnbull, Charlie Roberts (Captain), Harold Halse, Sandy Turnbull. Front row: Billy Meredith, George Wall. The trophies on the ground are the FA Charity Shield, Division One trophy and Manchester Cup.

◄ FA CUP FINAL

United captain Charlie Roberts – closely followed by Billy Meredith – leads his team out on to the pitch for the 1909 FA Cup Final against Bristol City. Both sides were debutants at this stage of the competition but United, having claimed their first Division One title the previous season, went into the match at Crystal Palace as favourites. They had not, however, enjoyed such a successful league campaign

during 1908-09 and would eventually finish a lowly 13th, 16 points behind champions Newcastle United.

▲ TURNBULL GOAL

After Harold Halse's shot had rebounded off the crossbar, Sandy Turnbull (out of picture) picks up the rebound to score what proved to be the only goal of the game in the 22nd minute. Bristol City goalkeeper Harry Clay can only look back in despair as the ball flies into the net. Halse and Meredith are the two United players watching the decisive action. Inside-left Turnbull's place in the team had been in jeopardy as he was struggling with a knee injury but Roberts convinced manager Ernest Mangnall to play him, stating: 'he might get a goal and if he does we can afford to carry him'.

FA CUP WINNERS 1909

CENTRAL STATION

Tens of thousands of enthusiastic supporters lined the streets of Manchester to welcome home their conquering heroes. Captain Charlie Roberts sits in the front of the coach proudly grasping the FA Cup trophy that was soon embroiled in a dispute between the club and the Football Association. To commemorate their historic victory, United commissioned a replica of the cup but the FA were not pleased and passed a resolution the following year dictating that the trophy could not be duplicated without their consent. As a result, a new cup was commissioned, created by Bradford jewellers Fattorini's and the design registered to protect it. This was to be the first in a long line of victory parades as Manchester United began their dominance of the FA Cup. By the end of 2011, the Old Trafford club would have appeared in a record-breaking 18 showpiece Finals, winning 11. The city-centre tour that began in an open horse-drawn carriage, however, would eventually be superseded by an open-top double-decker bus.

TODAY

Manchester Central was built between 1875 and 1880 by the Cheshire Lines Committee (CLC). The Midland Railway, one of the partners in the exercise, was then able to run expresses to London's St. Pancras station, as used by the United team. Passenger numbers dwindled in the Sixties and the station closed on 5 May 1969. For over a decade, Central Station fell derelict and its frontage was used as a car park. The site was acquired by Greater Manchester Council and in 1982 work began to convert it into the Greater Manchester Exhibition and Conference Centre or 'G-Mex', since renamed Manchester Central in a nod to its railway heritage.

FINAL AT MANCHESTER. "THE WINNING GOAL".   "WHO GOT THAT GOAL".

THE MOVE TO OLD TRAFFORD

◄ STADIUM FOR 80,000

It became evident that Bank Street was not a suitable ground for a League Championship and FA Cup-winning outfit so United searched for a new site, eventually choosing a piece of land on an industrial estate five miles away in the Borough of Stretford. Built at a cost of £90,000, Old Trafford's first game ended in a 4-3 defeat to Liverpool in February 1910. Boasting a capacity of some 80,000, the state-of-the-art arena was so impressive it was selected as the venue for the FA Cup Final Replay in 1911.

At the start of the 1911-12 season, reigning league champions United beat Southern League Champions Swindon Town 8-4 to lift the Charity Shield, their last trophy for many years. The slump in the Reds' fortunes began when manager Ernest Mangnall left, which in turn led to falling attendances. The situation was worsened by a match-fixing scandal in 1915. The suspension of football during World War I left the club with a costly new stadium to run with no revenue. United dropped into the Second Division in 1921-22, were promoted in 1925 but suffered relegation again in 1931. The Thirties saw the Reds continue as a 'yo-yo' side, bouncing back and forth between Divisions One and Two.

This aerial view of Old Trafford (left) from 1922 clearly shows the railway line running alongside the ground. The South Stand provides the only covered area in the stadium with the remaining three sides being left as earthwork terraces. Architect Archibald Leitch had written to the Cheshire Lines Committee trying to persuade them to subsidise the construction of the grandstand alongside the railway line but they declined. The CLC initially planned to build a new station next to the stadium but Trafford Park was eventually built further down the line. A timber platform was, however, opened next to the stadium in 1935.

▲ 1911 FA CUP FINAL

Old Trafford hosted its first showpiece match on 26 April 1911 when Newcastle United and Bradford City arrived for the FA Cup Final (above left). They had previously met four days earlier at Crystal Palace but neither side had been able to find the back of the net. At Old Trafford, however, Bantams captain Jimmy Speirs scored the only goal of the game in the 15th minute in front of a crowd of 58,000. It was to be the first in a host of games played at Old Trafford that did not involve United: the 1915 FA Cup Final saw Sheffield United beat Chelsea 3-0, watched by a mainly military crowd that led to the match being nicknamed 'the Khaki Cup Final'; while April 1926 saw the ground stage its first international match when England lost 1-0 to Scotland.

▲ 1921-22 TEAM

The 1921-22 squad (above right) that participated in one of the worst league campaigns in United's history are decked out in a mixture of home and change kits. The club had introduced matching red socks to the home kit the previous season while the change kit continued as a blue and white striped shirt, although the stripes were broader by 1921-22 than they had been prior to World War I.

VIEW FROM ABOVE
OLD TRAFFORD

◄ 1941 DAMAGE

This RAF photograph illustrates the aerial damage that had been inflicted on Old Trafford by Luftwaffe bombs aimed at the nearby docks and factories. The Main Stand has been demolished between the covered south-east and south-west quadrants but the tunnel withstood the bombardment. The stadium was hit during two raids – on 22 December 1940 and 11 March 1941.

The latter destroyed much of the stadium, including the Main Stand and forced United to leave their home while the club fought for compensation from the War Damage Commission. Having played their 'home' games at Maine Road in the interim, United finally returned to Old Trafford in August 1949. The first match was against Lancashire rivals Bolton Wanderers, the second fixture of the new campaign. It was a winning return to Old Trafford, with United running out 3-0 victors.

The aerial photo also shows 'the Railwaymen's' ongoing association with rail lines, with the Bridgewater Canal to the north of the stadium and the railway to the south – United's third stadium next to a railway.

▼ TODAY

The Trafford part of Manchester has seen much redevelopment in the second half of the twentieth century. Many of the industrial zones have suffered a similar fate to those all around the country as a plethora of retail parks has sprung up in their stead. One area of the Old Trafford stadium that has not been developed as much as the club would wish, however, is the single-tier South Stand. Its proximity to the railway line has limited any expansion plans although it had been regularly mooted that the club is looking into buying around 50 houses on the other side of the tracks so that a new stand – spanning the railway line – can be built. If this proposal ever comes to fruition, the increased capacity of the stadium would then be approximately 95,000...larger even than Wembley.

WORLD WAR II

THE DEPRESSION AND BEYOND

The death of John Henry Davies in 1927 had deepened the club's financial plight. Another local businessman, James W. Gibson, invested heavily in United in the early Thirties, but his lasting legacy was the foundation of the youth academy that reaped such rich rewards in the postwar era. Initially, though, his riches made little appreciable difference on the pitch. In 1934, the club fell to its lowest point, 20th place in Division Two, avoiding relegation to the Third Division by one point as local rivals Manchester City were winning the FA Cup with future Reds manager Matt Busby in the side. The balance of power in Manchester football began to shift when United were promoted in 1938, leapfrogging relegated City.

The outbreak of World War II in September 1939 caused the abandonment of the season after three games. Although Old Trafford still hosted football in the regional wartime competitions, it was requisitioned by the army for use as a depot. Alongside the heavy industry in the area, the stadium was a target for German bombing raids. Some

damage was sustained in December 1940 but football quickly resumed. A subsequent attack in March 1941 rendered Old Trafford unusable, destroying most of the main stand, some of the terraces and scorching the pitch (see opposite page).

▶ SERGEANT BUSBY

Many football players joined the armed forces during World War II to serve alongside the men who had spent their lives cheering their heroes from the terraces. Here, three international footballers – Joe Mercer (Everton), Matt Busby (Liverpool, but soon to become part of United folklore) and Don Welsh (Charlton Athletic) – proudly show off their Sergeants' stripes having enlisted in the army in 1939. Busby became a Company Sgt Major in the Ninth Battalion of the King's Liverpool Regiment.

▶ MANCHESTER BLITZED

King George VI inspects damage caused during an air raid in Piccadilly, Manchester, in February 1941. The Germans carried out a sustained period of bombing missions over Britain between 7 September 1940 and 10 May 1941 that became known as The Blitz. During a raid by the Luftwaffe on the night of 11 March 1941, Old Trafford took several direct hits as a result of bombs aimed at the nearby Vickers munitions factory and the Ford Motor Company, which had stopped assembling vehicles and was now manufacturing the Rolls-Royce Spitfire engines. When Louis Rocca persuaded the newly demobbed Matt Busby to manage the postwar United, he arrived to find the main grandstand in ruins, the wrecked terraces unmaintained and full of weeds; Nissen huts used for changing rooms and the training pitch a pile of rubble behind the Stretford End terrace. James W. Gibson stepped in again, and while negotiations went on with the government over compensation for war damage, he arranged a deal with Manchester City to rent Maine Road for a charge of £5,000 a season, plus 10 per cent of United's 'home' gate receipts.

BUSBY'S FIRST TROPHY

1948 FA CUP FINAL

A Liverpool player at the start of the war, Matt Busby was serving as a football coach in the Army Physical Training Corps in 1945. He had been offered a job as assistant manager at Liverpool when United snatched him from their Merseyside rivals. The Scot insisted on, and was given, full control of team selection and training and the signing of players without interference from the directors, something almost unheard-of in English football. He took up his duties in October 1945, recruiting army acquaintance Jimmy Murphy as right-hand man. Busby's

revolutionary approach quickly produced results with United finishing as runners-up in the league on resumption of the full programme in 1946-1947, followed by an FA Cup win over Blackpool in 1948.

The club's progress was all the more remarkable given that their home games had to be played at City's Maine Road stadium while Old Trafford was being rebuilt. United were stretched financially but with the assistance of grants from the War Damage Commission, Old Trafford was reopened, without cover to any of the stands, for the start of the 1949-1950 season, nearly 10 years since the last league game played there. Works to improve the stadium continued into the Fifties.

The photograph opposite shows King George VI meeting the Manchester United team before the 1948 FA Cup Final at Wembley. Blackpool had already announced their intention to play in their change strip of white shirts and black shorts to avoid a clash with the red shirts of the United players, but the FA instructed the Old Trafford side to wear their change strip of blue shirts and white shorts. This decision meant that neither side, unusually, would play the Final in their home kit.

▶ JOHN CAREY

United captain Johnny Carey is carried shoulder-high after his team beat Blackpool 4-2. It was United's first appearance in the Final for 39 years and the Red Devils were made to work for their victory. The Seasiders, though without their free-scoring Jimmy McIntosh, twice took the lead through Eddie Shimwell and Stan Mortensen before a brace from Jack Rowley levelled the match. Then one apiece from Stan Pearson and John Anderson sealed the win. Ironically, the two sides met four days later in a re-arranged league fixture with a solitary goal from McIntosh providing the FA Cup runners-up with a 1-0 victory at Bloomfield Road.

▶ LATE FORTIES / EARLY FIFTIES

Having finished as league runners-up in four out of five seasons from 1946-47 to 1950-51, United finally clinched the title in 1951-52. The side was captained by Irish full-back Johnny Carey and starred the exciting but controversial winger Charlie Mitten, prolific forwards Stan Pearson and Jack Rowley and left-back John Aston.

The seeds of the club's postwar success were sown by Chairman James W. Gibson when he created United's Junior Athletic Club – a forerunner of today's academies – to bring on local talent. As testimony to Gibson's vision, when United carried off the FA Cup in 1948, four of the forward line – Jack Rowley, Johnny Morris, Stan Pearson and Charlie Mitten – had been brought up in Manchester.

The following three campaigns saw United as a team in transition, struggling to make an impact on the race for honours. Carey's retirement at the end of 1952–53 came amid manager Matt Busby's remoulding of the side, the heroes of the immediate postwar period being replaced not by big-money signings but by young players.

Duncan Edwards was typical of Busby's new philosophy. Pictured right shaking the hand of United coach Jimmy Murphy after making his league debut against Cardiff in April 1953, he would go on to become the core of the 'Busby Babes'. Edwards, who was sixteen and a half at the time, was still playing for the United Youth side. Busby would also give debuts to youngsters Dennis Viollet and Jackie Blanchflower that season.

THE 'BABES' ERA

◀ QUEUES ON RAILWAY ROAD

United fans queue in the street for tickets for the FA Cup Fifth Round clash with Portsmouth in February 1950. The unusual scenes in Railway Road were a clear indication of the increasing popularity of Matt Busby's team. The previously well-ordered queue – which had extended down the right-hand side of the road – was in danger of becoming a potentially life-threatening stampede. The match itself proved an exciting affair that ended in a 3-3 draw at Old Trafford courtesy of goals from Charlie Mitten (2) and Stan Pearson. The replay at Fratton Park saw Pompey defeated 3-1 with goals from Jimmy Delaney, John Downie and Mitten. The cup run ended, however, in the sixth round with a 2-0 defeat at Chelsea.

▶ YOUTH POLICY

Matt Busby talks to a group of young footballers – including (from left to right) Duncan Edwards, Jackie Blanchflower and Dennis Viollet – at Old Trafford in January 1954. By the early Fifties, Busby's established team were aging and demanding higher wages that the club were reluctant to agree to. Many of these players were sold to other clubs and he, therefore, set up a system for bringing youth players through the ranks. It proved a revelation for United as the 'Busby Babes' – as they were nicknamed by the press – were about to launch the club on a new era of domination.

CHAMPIONS 1955-56

Busby's gradual integration of young players was a phenomenal success as United were runaway Champions in 1955-56 by an 11-point margin, retaining the title the following season. The team had an average age of 22. Tommy Taylor, signed from Barnsley, was leading scorer for both seasons with goals coming from Dennis Viollet and, during 1956-57, Liam Whelan and Bobby Charlton who were both breaking into the senior side. Only Roger Byrne and Johnny Berry had played in the Championship-winning side of 1952.

Defeat by Aston Villa in the 1957 Cup Final denied the club the cup and league double, a feat that had not been achieved since 1897. United played for much of the game without goalkeeper Ray Wood who required treatment for a broken jaw. Jackie Blanchflower deputised and the Reds eventually went down 2-1.

The fame of the 'Busby Babes' increased, as they became the first English entrants to the European Cup, defying the Football League who feared it would adversely affect domestic fixtures. Now in its second season, the competition pitted the champions of European national leagues against each other in a two-legged knockout format. United reached the 1957 Semi-Finals, losing to eventual winners Real Madrid.

▲ TODAY

Railway Road has long ceased to host fans queueing for tickets. With demand continually outstripping supply it is only the fringe games that provide the opportunity for the casual sale.

MRS WATSON'S OLD TRAFFORD GUEST HOUSE

◀ A CURE FOR HOMESICKNESS

Matt Busby had long believed in the ethos that if he brought players in while they were young, he could train them to play the way he thought would bring most success and mould them into model professionals. He gathered a team around him – including Jimmy Murphy, Bert Whalley and Joe Armstrong – that would enable the club to scout the best footballing schoolboys from around the country (and even across the Irish Sea) and nurture their talent. It was by these means that the talents of Eddie Colman, Duncan Edwards, David Pegg and Bobby Charlton had been nurtured.

One of Busby's major concerns when it came to nurturing young talent was the boys' emotional welfare. With this in mind, a number of local residents were interviewed as the Forties ran into the new decade to find suitable places for the youngsters to lodge. His belief was that if they had a suitable family home environment while they established themselves then they were less likely to suffer from homesickness. The system soon reaped dividends as the United team that claimed the 1955-56 First Division title had an average age of just 22, the youngest ever to achieve that feat.

Many of the Busby Babes are seen left sitting around the table in Mrs Watson's guest house near Old Trafford in September 1953. Clockwise, from bottom left: Tommy Taylor, Mrs Watson, Bobby Charlton, Liam Whelan, Winnie, Jackie Blanchflower, Mark Jones, Gordon Clayton, Joan, Alan Rhodes and Duncan Edwards. It was a typical scene in the lives of the young Manchester United players, many of whom had yet to make their first-team debut.

▶ THE PLAZA BALLROOM

Matt Busby lived up to his fatherly image by making sure that each of his apprentices learnt a trade, just in case their footballing career didn't work out. When not sharpening his football skills, Charlton worked as an apprentice at Switchgear & Cowans, an engineering firm (still in business today) close to his digs.

Their week's training finished, the lads were free to indulge themselves and go into town on Saturday nights. One of their familiar haunts was the Plaza Ballroom (shown top right in the Forties). They would get the bus or get a lift in David Pegg's Morris Minor or Tommy Taylor's Vauxhall Victor. At the Plaza, the then manager Jimmy Savile, would arrange a quiet table away from over-enthusiastic autograph hunters. Living and playing together helped bond the Busby babes and forge a strong spirit, with the motherly Mrs Watson keeping an eye on what they got up to.

Today the walls of the Plaza Ballroom no longer reverberate to the hit sounds spun by Jimmy Savile and Dave Lee Travis, two house DJs of earlier times. The site was redeveloped in 1998 as a branch of JD Wetherspoon's.

MUNICH: BEFORE

MATCH BUILD-UP

Competing in the European Cup again in 1957-58, United's exciting young side were many people's favourites to end Real Madrid's domination of the tournament. Matches were held midweek with Football League games on Saturdays. Air travel remained the only realistic option when the club was drawn against Eastern European opposition.

After overcoming Shamrock Rovers and Dukla Prague, United faced Red Star Belgrade in the Quarter-Finals. United won the home leg 2-1 in January 1958, leaving the tie delicately poised. After experiencing debilitating delays returning

from the Prague fixture, Matt Busby decided to charter an aircraft through British European Airways for the second leg of the Quarter-Final in Belgrade on 5 February 1958. The United contingent prepared to board their airplane at Ringway Airport for the trip to Belgrade in the knowledge that several of the players – who were accompanied on the trip by journalists and club officials – were understandably anxious about venturing behind the Iron Curtain, mainly due to frequent reports of persecution in the Communist state.

▲ THE HISTORIC LINE-UP

The final picture of the Busby Babes as the team line up on the pitch for the second leg of their European Cup Quarter-Final against Red Star Belgrade on 5 February 1958. From left to right: Duncan Edwards, Eddie Colman, Mark Jones, Kenny Morgans, Bobby Charlton, Dennis Viollet, Tommy Taylor, Bill Foulkes, Harry Gregg, Albert Scanlon and Roger Byrne. The team were on a 10-match unbeaten run in all competitions and were progressing well in the league, FA Cup and European Cup.

► CHARLTON GOAL

A crowd of 52,000 at Belgrade's JNA Stadium saw United race to a three-goal lead in half an hour. Dennis Viollet opened the scoring after two minutes and Bobby Charlton added two more in rapid succession. The away goals rule left their hosts with an uphill task. Red Star fought back in the second half with Kostic netting shortly after the break and Tasic adding the second from the penalty spot four minutes later. Kostic's equaliser two minutes from time was little more than a consolation. United were in the Semi-Finals.

MUNICH: THE CRASH

6 FEBRUARY 1958

The return flight from Belgrade's Zemun Airport on 6 February 1958 was delayed for an hour because Johnny Berry had mislaid his passport. Commanded by co-pilots Captains Thane and Rayment, BEA's Elizabethan class Airspeed Ambassador registration G-ALZU and named 'Lord Burghley' landed at a snow-bound Munich Airport at 13:15 GMT for a scheduled refuelling. After two take-off attempts were aborted because of technical problems with the engines, the passengers disembarked, returning to the lounge.

It was now snowing heavily, leading some of the United party to assume that the flight would be delayed until the next day. Having overcome the engine problems, the co-pilots decided to make a third take-off attempt. Barely 15 minutes after getting off the plane, the increasingly apprehensive passengers were summoned back.

Shortly after three o'clock that afternoon, the plane proceeded along the runway, left the ground briefly then skidded off the end of the runway, crashed through the airport fence and across a road. Its port wing struck a house and part of the plane's tail was torn off. The cockpit hit a tree and the right side of the fuselage collided with a wooden hut containing fuel which exploded. The plane had split in two. Of the 38 passengers, 20 people died immediately; three others died later. Fatalities included eight United players.

▲ WRECKAGE

The wreckage of British European Airways' Flight 609 at Munich Airport. The Airspeed AS57 Ambassador was a twin piston-engined airliner developed in the late Forties that proved popular due to its pressurised cabin and effective soundproofing. BEA ordered 20 such aircraft in 1948 and they were operational between 1952 and 1958. As well as its notorious link to the Munich Air Disaster of 1958, an Ambassador was also involved in a fatal incident at Heathrow Airport 10 years later when a transport model crashed, killing all but two members of its crew as well as several horses and their accompanying grooms.

▶ CHARLTON RECOVERS

Bobby Charlton lies in his hospital bed recuperating from the injuries he suffered in the crash. Unlike many of his team-mates, Charlton was not seriously injured and would return to first-team action less than a month later, appearing in the FA Cup sixth round encounter with West Bromwich Albion that ended in a 2-2 draw.

MUNICH: A NATION IN SHOCK

FOOTBALL'S DARKEST NIGHT

As news of events in Munich reached Britain, it assumed the status of national tragedy, with an outpouring of sympathy for young lives so cruelly cut short. Geoff Bent (25), Roger Byrne (28), Eddie Colman (21), Mark Jones (24), David Pegg (22), Tommy Taylor (26) and Liam 'Billy' Whelan (22) were killed instantly. Duncan Edwards (21), the shining star of his generation, would die two weeks later. Nine players survived, although two would never play again. Johnny Berry awoke with no memory of the crash during which he sustained a fractured skull, jaw, elbow, pelvis and leg, injuries which meant that he never played football again. Jackie Blanchflower also suffered fractures to his pelvis, arms and legs, along with crushed kidneys. His brave attempts to resume his playing career were unsuccessful.

Eighteen-year old Kenny Morgans, the youngest footballer involved in the disaster, was never the same player afterwards and left United in 1961. Albert Scanlon, Dennis Viollet and Ray Wood all went on to play for United again but were subsequently transferred to other clubs. Busby rebuilt the team around a trio of Munich survivors, Bill Foulkes, Harry Gregg and Bobby Charlton, who were fortunate enough to escape with relatively minor injuries. Foulkes had been sitting at the point where the aircraft split in two and was able to free himself and help the rescue effort. Charlton, along with Viollet, had swapped seats with Tommy Taylor and David Pegg who believed that the back of the plane was safer.

◀ FINAL JOURNEY

German officials – including Sepp Herberger, coach of the national football team; Ludwig Maierboeck, manager of the Bavarian Football Association; and Hans Huber, vice-president of the German Football Association – watch as coffins containing the bodies of 21 victims of the crash leave Munich's Riem airport. A West German police guard give their honour salute as the flight departs. The Vickers Viscount airliner was repatriating the deceased to a country shocked by the events that had unfurled on 6 February 1958. Fans lined the streets to pay their respects when the bodies were brought back to Manchester, heading for Old Trafford in a lengthy cortege. A crowd of more than 200,000 mourners waited in the rain as the delayed flight from Munich landed, by which time the streets all the way from Ringway to the ground were lined three deep in places by supporters of both the city's clubs.

▶ A CITY MOURNS

The United funeral cortege returns to Manchester on 10 February 1958. News of the crash had quickly reverberated around Manchester with Mark Jones' wife, finding out about the tragedy in a local supermarket. Meanwhile, the telegram that Duncan Edwards had sent to his landlady following the second aborted take-off – that stated 'All flights cancelled. Flying tomorrow. Duncan' – arrived after news of the crash had been received. United had been due to play Wolverhampton Wanderers that Saturday, February 8, but Old Trafford remained empty while the sport stood in silent tribute. Clubs all over the country and, indeed, Europe paid homage to the dead with a pre-match minute's silence.

▶ CHARLTON LEAVES HOSPITAL

Bobby Charlton with Valerie Mollard and Dr Sigrid Jaaks at a thank-you reception for medical staff at Munich Hospital. Charlton suffered cuts as well as severe shock and recuperated in the hospital for a week before heading back to England. He spent the next few weeks convalescing with family in Ashington before returning to Old Trafford, where expectations were high that the youngster would play an integral part in rebuilding the club.

BUSBY'S RECOVERY

Manager Matt Busby sustained severe damage to his legs and spent two months in hospital fighting for his life; he was given the Last Rites twice. Blaming himself for the crash, he considered quitting football until his wife Jean intervened. Busby resumed managerial duties for the start of the 1958-59 season.

Speculation was rife that Manchester United would fold, but Busby's assistant Jimmy Murphy, whose other job as manager of Wales had prevented him travelling, took charge of team affairs.

MUNICH: THE INVESTIGATION

◄ ELEVEN YEARS LATER

The aircraft in the sky reveals how close to the end of the runway Flight 609 came down. At first, it was believed that the Munich air disaster was caused by pilot error, particularly as the German airport authorities prosecuted surviving co-pilot Captain Thane, alleging that he had neglected to de-ice the wings before take-off. Eleven years later, Thane's name was cleared by a British investigation which concluded that the build up of slush on the runway had prevented the aircraft from taking off at the correct speed and that this was the responsibility of the airport.

The United charter flight included representatives of the British press, eight of whom died, amongst them former Manchester City and England goalkeeper turned *News of the World* journalist Frank Swift. Three members of the club's staff perished – long-serving secretary Walter Crickmer, trainer Tom Curry and chief coach Bert Whalley.

After regaining consciousness, goalkeeper Harry Gregg had kicked his way out of the aircraft, and although urged to flee by the crew who feared an explosion, he heard a baby's cry and returned to rescue 22-month old Vesna Lukic and her pregnant mother Vera, the wife of a Yugoslavian diplomat. Gregg then pulled Bobby Charlton and Dennis Viollet away from the wreckage, mistakenly believing them to be dead, and helped the seriously injured Matt Busby and Jackie Blanchflower get clear.

▲ TODAY

A new memorial to those who lost their lives in the Munich Air Disaster was unveiled in Germany on 22 September 2004. Funded by Manchester United, the granite plaque set in sandstone expresses the club's gratitude to those who helped care for the injured. The unveiling ceremony was attended by Bobby Charlton, Alex Ferguson and Chief Executive David Gill.

In April 2008, the Munich town council decided to rename the site where the memorial stands Manchesterplatz in recognition of the ties that bind the two cities. Manchesterplatz is in the vicinity of the old airport, on the corner of Reppenweg and Emplstrasse in the village of Kirchtrudering. Riem was the main international airport of Munich until it was closed in May 1992, the day before a new airport near Freising commenced operation.

MUNICH: MEMORIAL

◄ THE FIRST PLAQUE

Matt Busby unveils the first memorial at Old Trafford on 25 February 1960 in a ceremony attended by the relatives of those who had died, survivors of the crash and members of the present team. The plaque – located above the entrance to the directors' box – was in the shape of a football pitch and bears the names of the victims in black and gold glass. The teak carving above this is in the shape of a player and a supporter, both with their heads bowed, either side of a wreath. As the stadium was remodelled in the Seventies, however, the position of this plaque became untenable but it was not possible to remove the memorial without causing irreparable damage. A decision was therefore taken to wall up the original plaque in the Main Stand and install a slate replacement that appeared in 1976. This was itself replaced by a third version (opposite) at the same time as a statue of Sir Matt Busby was erected in 1996.

▼ FOR SERVICES TO FOOTBALL

In recognition of his services to football, Matt Busby was awarded a CBE in July 1958. He collected the honour at Buckingham Palace with wife Jean and son Sandy. Ten years later he would be back for a knighthood.

▲ THE MUNICH CLOCK

The Munich Clock at Old Trafford is another constant reminder of the tragedy in February 1958. Funded by the Ground Committee, the simple two-faced clock on the south-east corner of the stadium is stopped at 3.04pm – the time of the crash – during memorials to remember the players, staff and other passengers who lost their lives. There have been ceremonies in recent years on the 40th and 50th anniversaries but the clock has also been the focal point of fans' grief on other occasions as well, such as the death of Sir Matt Busby on 20 January 1994.

DUNCAN EDWARDS

FOOTBALL PRODIGY

Duncan Edwards was born in Dudley on 1 October 1936. His performances for the English Schools XI attracted the attention of several major football clubs. United won the battle for his signature. He made his First Division debut in April 1951; at 16 years 185 days, he remains the youngest player to play top flight football in England. The photograph left shows Edwards training in August 1954. In April 1955, he earned his first England cap and was, for over forty years, the country's youngest international. He played 18 times for the national side and was an integral part of the United side which won the league title in 1955-56 and 1956-57.

After the Munich air disaster, Edwards was taken to hospital with multiple leg fractures, broken ribs and seriously damaged kidneys. Had he recovered, it was unlikely that he would have played again. After a two-week fight for life, Edwards succumbed to kidney failure, dying on 21 February 1958. While Duncan Edwards was fighting for his life in hospital, a new issue of Charles Buchan's *Football Monthly* was published in the United Kingdom bearing a photograph of a smiling Edwards on the cover. Doctors had initially been cautiously hopeful that, despite his multiple injuries, Edwards would recover but it was unlikely that he would ever play football again. As it turned out, however, the artificial kidney that was rushed to the hospital had a detrimental effect on his blood's clotting ability and he suffered with internal bleeding before losing his fight for life 15 days after the crash.

FIRST TEAM REGULAR AT 17

Edwards was a complete footballer. Possessed of a muscular physique, he was a powerful tackler, adept at passing and shooting with either foot. Although usually a defensive wing-half, he was comfortable in any outfield position. The football world mourned, and continues to mourn, the loss of one of the most talented players to grace the English game.

In the 1954-55 season he established himself as a first-team regular, finishing the campaign with 36 appearances and six goals as United finished fifth in the First Division. The league title – last won in 1951-52 – soon returned to Old Trafford, however, with back-to-back trophies in 1955-56 and 1956-57.

TIPPED AS FUTURE ENGLAND CAPTAIN

Edwards had been in a fantastic run of form as the 1957-58 season got under way – so much so that there were rumours regarding interest from top Italian clubs – and it was widely anticipated that he would be an integral part of England's World Cup challenge the following year in Sweden. He was also tipped to take over the captaincy of his country from the ageing Billy Wright.

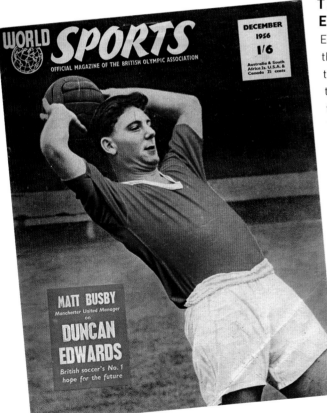

▲ HONOURED

Duncan Edwards was buried in Dudley Cemetery on 26 February 1958, alongside his sister Carol, with thousands lining the streets in mourning. The tombstone is a mecca to many United fans who pass through the area. There are numerous memorials to Edwards in his home town in the West Midlands including this statue in the town centre that was dedicated in 1999 by Edwards' mother and Bobby Charlton.

1958 CUP FINAL

UNLUCKY LOSERS

It could quite easily be mistaken for a victory parade, such was the turnout on 4 May 1958 for the return of the Manchester United team from their FA Cup Final date at Wembley, a 2-0 defeat to Bolton Wanderers.

Matt Busby's assistant Jimmy Murphy had the arduous task of organising a team for the first match following Munich. United had been given leave to postpone their FA Cup Fifth Round tie at home to Sheffield Wednesday until 19 February but, such was the turmoil that the club found itself in, there were no players listed in the home team line-up when the match programme was printed.

Murphy had drafted in Stan Crowther from Aston Villa and Ernie Taylor from Blackpool but – apart from two others – the remainder of the team was made up of reserves and youth team players. The first two names on the team sheet,

however, were Munich survivors captain Bill Foulkes and goalkeeper Harry Gregg and their appearance on the Old Trafford pitch drew roars of support from the crowd.

Buoyed by the emotion, United scored three times without reply – including two from debutant Shay Brennan – and went on to overcome the challenge of West Brom and Fulham (both after replays) to book their place in the Final.

Mounted police cleared the way for the open-top bus to make its way down London Road as the residents of Manchester welcomed their heroes home. Emotions were running high and many felt that it didn't really matter that the FA Cup had not been won for a third consecutive year – the players had done their fans and their city proud simply by reaching the Final less than three months after Munich.

▶ HARRY GREGG INJURY

Players, officials and touchline staff gather around United's goalkeeper Harry Gregg after the collision with Bolton striker Nat Lofthouse in the 1958 FA Cup Final. Gregg had become the world's most expensive goalkeeper when he signed from Doncaster Rovers the previous December in a £23,500 deal but even he could not prevent Bolton doubling their lead, albeit in controversial circumstances. Lofthouse – who had opened the scoring in the third minute – had charged into Gregg, knocking him unconscious and bundled him and the ball into the net. Even the 'Lion of Vienna', as Lofthouse was known, was amazed the goal was allowed to stand. United were unable to reply and the Trotters won 2-0.

JIMMY MURPHY

Born in 1910 in Pentre, Wales, Jimmy Murphy enjoyed a long career as an accomplished wing-half with West Brom and had played in the 1935 FA Cup Final, losing 4-2 against Sheffield Wednesday. He moved to Swindon Town in 1938 but

the outbreak of World War II brought a premature end to his playing career. He came to the attention of Matt Busby while giving a speech about football to serving troops and, such was his passion and knowledge, that Busby made Murphy his first signing when he accepted the position of Manchester United manager. As assistant manager, Murphy was charged with transforming promising young footballers into talented professionals and he excelled in this role until he retired in 1971.

On duty with the Wales team at the time of the Munich crash, Murphy was uncomfortable in the limelight and preferred to stay as Busby's right-hand man rather than seeking glory in his own managerial position. The much-loved Welshman was honoured after his death in 1989 when United commissioned the 'Jimmy Murphy Young Player of the Year Award', to be given to the best player in the club's youth system.

▶ TODAY

Much of Manchester has been remodelled over recent decades and Piccadilly Station is no exception. The Grade 2 listed train-shed roof was completely rebuilt towards the close of the 20th century and in 2001-02 the remainder of the station was rebuilt to cater for the expected influx of visitors to the 2002 Commonwealth Games.

MATT BUSBY

▲ BUSBY, THE PLAYER

Matt Busby introduces Winston Churchill's wife Clementine to members of his Scottish team before a match against England at Wembley in January 1942 for the Aid to Russia Fund. The visiting team included another man who would go on to become a legend in English football management and, indeed, Busby's keenest rival in England's top division. Bill Shankly (third from the right) orchestrated Liverpool's rise to the top while manager at the Anfield club from 1959 until 1974.

◄ BUSBY, THE TRAINER

Matt Busby takes charge of a team training session in March 1957. When Busby took over at Old Trafford, he insisted on being in charge of every aspect of the first team. This included deciding which players he bought and sold without interference from the directors, picking his own starting 11 and leading the players in their daily training routines. It bucked the normal trend in English football, but proved to be a huge success for the club and a trendsetting move in the modern game.

► BUSBY, THE MANAGER

Matt Busby plots United's domination of English football. Having officially taken over as manager on 1 October 1945, Busby's initial assessment of the club was that he would need five years for his efforts to come to fruition. With United having been in the doldrums of the Second Division in the years before the war, he immediately led the club to their highest league finish since the title-winning 1910-11 season and his team were regularly runners-up in the First Division before they claimed their first Championship in 1951-52.

CAREER DETAILS: Matt Busby was born into a coal-mining family in Bellshill, Scotland, on 26 May 1909 but made his name in England after signing for Manchester City at the age of 17. Citing his heroes as the legendary Alex James (Arsenal and Scotland) and Hughie Gallacher (Newcastle United and Scotland), Busby went on to make more than 200 appearances for the Maine Road club, winning the FA Cup in 1934, before transferring to Liverpool for £8,000 in 1936. While at Anfield, Busby struck up a lifelong friendship with future Liverpool manager, Bob Paisley.

As with many footballers of this era, World War II curtailed his playing career and Busby signed on as a football coach in the Army Physical Training Corps. After the hostilities ended, he accepted the post of Manchester United manager.

He won his first silverware in 1948 when his side defeated Blackpool 4-2 in the FA Cup Final and went on to claim three Division One titles in the Fifties before his squad was decimated in the Munich Air Disaster. He returned to Old Trafford and guided his charges to the 1963 FA Cup with a 3-1 win over Leicester City. But his primary goals were reclaiming the First Division crown and conquering Europe, a quest he first began in 1956 with a 12-0 aggregate victory over Anderlecht. Having finished as runners-up to Liverpool at the end of the 1963-64 season, Busby's team – now including the 'Holy Trinity' of Bobby Charlton, Denis Law and George Best – went one better the following year...but only just! A 2-1 defeat in the final match of the campaign saw United finish on 61 points, the same as Leeds United, but they claimed their first Division One crown since 1956-57 with a better goal average than their Yorkshire rivals. A disappointing fourth position finish in 1965-66 was coupled with Semi-Final anguish – a 1-0 loss to Everton in the FA Cup and 2-1 on aggregate to Partizan Belgrade in the European Cup – before the league title returned to Old Trafford the following season, enabling Busby to launch another offensive on Europe (see page 116).

► BUSBY, THE INSPIRATION

Matt Busby was always happy to take young managers under his wing – none more so than fellow Scot Tommy Docherty, then manager of Chelsea and at 33 the youngest in the league. The pair are pictured playing snooker at the Norbreck Hydro in Blackpool in 1962. 'The Doc' of course would take over at Old Trafford in 1972 and said 'I think I needled Matt by getting rid of some players past their best,' presumably referring to Old Trafford legends George Best and Denis Law.

HOME AFTER MUNICH

TIME TO REBUILD

Matt Busby returns home after 10 weeks in the Rechts der Isar Hospital in Munich. He owed his life to Professor Georgs Muhrer and his dedicated team. He was not aware of the extent of the tragedy until some weeks after the crash, as doctors felt he was not strong enough to be told the truth.

Wife Jean travelled to Germany to accompany her husband home on the ferry via the Hook of Holland and Harwich. It was supposed to be a quiet homecoming for Busby, who was using crutches due to an injured leg, but the media scrum around his house on his return was made worse by wellwishers. Busby handed team affairs over to his able assistant, Jimmy Murphy, who not only had the task

of rebuilding the United squad, but was manager of the Welsh national team competing in the 1958 World Cup in Sweden. It was Wales' only appearance in the competition and consequently the only World Cup where all four home nations – England, Scotland, Northern Ireland and Wales – would take part. Busby watched as much of the tournament as he could on television as he recuperated at home. Goalkeeper Harry Gregg was there representing Northern Ireland, Bobby Charlton was the only United player in the England squad, while little-known forward Colin Webster turned out for Wales. Busby watched and took notes.

TODAY

Busby's modest house reflected the remuneration for the job. Managers' salaries were rarely reported in the press at the time, but his 'Busby Babes', a phrase he detested, would have been earning around £20 a week in 1958. At the same time, you could buy a Manchester United jersey for 22 shillings (excluding postage). He liked to keep his players close to him. While the Babes were lodged with Mrs

Watson, the married players were given houses nearby that they rented from the club for £3 a week. These days, with Sir Alex Ferguson on an annual salary believed to be around the £4 million mark, the likelihood that the Manchester United manager resides in similarly modest accommodation is slim to none.

SIR MATT BUSBY: EUROPEAN CUP

◄ RETURN TO WEMBLEY

He had played there for Scotland and led his team out for FA Cup Finals, but this was a bigger stage for the former Liverpool and Man City player. Matt Busby cannot resist getting a feel for the Wembley pitch before the 1968 European Cup Final. This was the first time his team had reached the showpiece event, having fallen at the Semi-Final hurdle every time they had qualified for the competition (in 1956-57, 1957-58 and 1965-66). It was the first time that the Final had been staged at Wembley Stadium and the United team of 2010-11 returned to the scene of the club's first European triumph when they took on Barcelona.

◄ 2011

Like his predecessor, former Rangers player Alex Ferguson continues to take an active role in training with United. He is photographed inset during a training session prior to United's Champions League Semi-Final first leg against Schalke in April 2011. His team secured a 2-0 advantage in the away leg and ensured their progress to their third Final in four years – a rematch of the 2009 Final that Barcelona won 2-0 – with an emphatic 4-1 victory at Old Trafford, despite fielding a shadow side. While Ferguson had already overtaken Busby's record in the premier European competition by winning the trophy in 1999 and 2008, he was aiming to become only the second manager (thereby emulating Liverpool's Bob Paisley) to register three wins in the Champions League/European Cup. (The competition was renamed on its reorganisation in 1992.)

► LONG OVERDUE

Matt Busby poses with the European Cup at Old Trafford at the start of the 1968-69 season. Many have argued that this trophy should have been United's long before, but the events of Munich a decade earlier forced Busby to rebuild his decimated team. Having achieved his dream of conquering Europe, Busby went on to become the longest-serving manager in the club's history before being overtaken by Sir Alex Ferguson on 19 December 2010. The two Old Trafford legends also have the distinction of being the only Manchester United managers to receive a knighthood.

▼ 1999

Alex Ferguson poses in the foyer of his hotel with his first European Cup, won in dramatic fashion the night before against Bayern Munich.

SIR MATT BUSBY: LEGACY

PASSING INTO LEGEND

Sir Matt Busby is recognised as having created three great Manchester United teams, one in each decade between the Forties and Sixties, as he transformed the club into one of Europe's finest. His was the benchmark that every subsequent United manager has had to live up to and his name and legacy live on in the 21st century.

Sir Matt's replacement was former Busby Babe Wilf McGuinness, whose playing career had been cut short with a broken leg at 22. McGuinness, a former England Under-23 manager, took over first-team responsibility in June 1969, but the directors were not pleased with the direction the club was heading in and, on his dismissal in December 1970, persuaded Matt Busby to come out of retirement in a caretaker role for the remainder of the season. Busby continued as a director before being appointed Club President in 1982 and was a familiar face at Old Trafford until his death in January 1994 at the age of 84. Many tried – and ultimately failed – to emulate his success and it wasn't until the arrival of Alex Ferguson in November 1986 that the club finally found a manager who would end up serving more than five years in the post.

▲ IN MOURNING

Old Trafford is swamped under a sea of scarves and flowers as fans mourn the death of Sir Matt Busby on 20 January 1994 at the age of 84. In spite of the fact that Busby retired 23 years earlier, fans still held him in reverence as United's most successful manager. While the Scot lived long enough to see his beloved club end their 26-year league title drought in 1992-93, United did not win their second European Cup (by then renamed the Champions League) until what would have been Busby's 90th birthday, 26 May 1999. Busby was awarded the CBE in 1958 and was knighted following the European Cup victory in 1968. A devout Catholic, he was made a Knight Commander of St Gregory by the Pope in 1972.

He had served United as a director for 13 years before being made club president in 1982, and 20 years later was made an inaugural inductee of the English Football Hall of Fame in recognition of the mark he made on the English game.

► TODAY

A bronze statue of Sir Matt Busby erected in 1995 keeps a watchful eye over Old Trafford. Located on the exterior of the East Stand above the Megastore, the statue, designed by sculptor Philip Jackson, overlooks Sir Matt Busby Way, as well as a statue of his United Trinity – Messrs Best, Law and Charlton – who were instrumental in his ultimate triumph.

Oscar-like statuettes of the Busby statue are now used as trophies in the annual club award scheme. Wayne Rooney has his own 'Busby' at home for winning the Sir Matt Busby Player of the Year award in 2005-06 and 2009-10.

TRAVEL BY PLANE
HARDAKER'S HARDLINE ATTITUDE

The Football Association and the Football League were never keen on European competitions and had successfully put pressure on Chelsea not to compete in the inaugural 1955-56 European Cup tournament.

When Busby did enter Manchester United in the European Cup, it was on the understanding that they return to England at least 24 hours before their next league fixture, which was then against the eventual champions, Wolverhampton Wanderers.

'Alan Hardaker (the then secretary of the Football League) argued that he was protecting the "integrity" of the league, preventing important matches being squeezed into the programme in the shadow of European action,' Charlton wrote in his autobiography. 'Another interpretation was that he was making it as difficult as possible for the man (Busby) who had defied him with his insistence that United would fight on this new frontier of football.'

Pictured here, the United team prepare to leave London in August 1959 to fly to Munich for a friendly against Bayern. The trip also included a visit to the hospital that had been so instrumental in their recent history where they were fondly greeted as old friends, with the crash survivors giving huge bouquets of flowers to the staff. Despite being reduced to nine men, United won the match 2-1.

► FIRST SEASON IN EUROPE

Manchester United secretary Walter Crickmer greets the Atletico Bilbao squad at Manchester's Ringway Airport in February 1957. Matt Busby and his players had endured a difficult trip to Portugal the previous month where bad weather had forced the pilot to circle the airport for 20 minutes in gale-force winds which resulted in Duncan Edwards suffering airsickness. The first half of the European Cup Quarter-Final in Lisbon proved to be a disaster with the home side taking a 3-0 lead at half-time. But United rallied after the interval to finish the match 5-3 losers. On arrival at the barely equipped Bilbao Airport on the Thursday morning, the pilot announced the flight would be cancelled unless sufficient volunteers could be found to sweep ice off the wings. The return leg in Manchester saw unanswered goals from Johnny Berry, Tommy Taylor and Dennis Viollet book a place in the Semi-Final against Real Madrid.

▼ TODAY

Traffic at Manchester Airport has increased rapidly since World War II and it is now the fourth busiest in the UK. United will invariably travel back the same night of the fixture. While the early days of European competition only involved a maximum of five trips abroad (depending on where the Final was held), the 2010-11 structure of the Champions League meant up to 11 matches abroad if they were to compete in every stage of the tournament. In 2006 they went one step better than any other Premiership club by revealing their own Manchester United branded plane, a part of the Air Asia fleet.

TRAVEL BY RAIL

◄ PASSING THE TIME

Most away games, apart from 'local' derbies, meant overnight stays due to the distance from Manchester and it was common for the club to send the team by rail to games that involved long journeys as it was the most effective means of travel. Changes were afoot, however, that would increase the amount of travel that teams undertook by coach. The first section of motorway was the Preston Bypass (opened in 1958 and now part of the M6) while the M1 between Crick and Berrygrove was the first of many major motorways built in the second half of the 20th century. Indeed, in the early Sixties the government set itself a target of creating 1,000 miles of motorway by the end of that decade.

The Sixties also saw changes to the country's railway as British Railways went about modernising the network with diesel and electric locomotives taking over from the traditional steam.

In the photo top left, the United players – from left to right: Wilf McGuinness, Bill Foulkes, Mark Jones, Eddie Colman and Ray Wood – are heading to Bournemouth in March 1957. In Bournemouth, United won the FA Cup sixth round tie 2-1 with a brace of goals from Johnny Berry before seeing off the challenge of Birmingham City in the Semi-Final. Alas, Busby's team were unable to complete the Double by adding the FA Cup to the Division One title they had won, eight points clear of second-placed Spurs.

◄ MANCHESTER PICCADILLY

Denis Law walks along the platform at Piccadilly Railway Station, carrying his suitcase as he prepares to board a train in 1963. Previously named London Road Station, it was rechristened Manchester Piccadilly when it was reopened on 12 September 1960 after renovations for the new London Midland Region electric train services to London. It is still today many visitors' first taste of Manchester with its original iron sheds and decorative columns that date from the 1880s.

INTER-CITY SPEED

Seen here in May 1968, United's World Cup winners Bobby Charlton and Nobby Stiles while away their journey to London with a few games of cribbage. While travel to away games had always been notoriously arduous due to the length of the journeys, the Sixties saw new innovations slash the amount of time it took to travel long distances. British Rail launched their new Inter-City trains in 1966 as part of its electrification of the major part of the West Coast Main Line, notably new express services between London and the major cities of Manchester, Birmingham and Liverpool.

Above right, trainer Jack Crompton and Denis Law enjoy the luxury of first-class travel on the train back to Manchester in May 1963. The Scottish striker had been on the scoresheet – along with David Herd – as United defeated Leicester City in the FA Cup Final to claim their first trophy of the Sixties. Needless to say, smoking in trains is prohibited today, while few sportsmen – Wayne Rooney aside – have been pictured enjoying a cigarette.

AYTOUN STREET

STANDING ROOM ONLY

For many years, a familiar match day sight in Manchester was the long line of double-deckers in Aytoun Street, near Piccadilly Gardens, waiting to ferry supporters to Old Trafford (or Maine Road). Manchester Corporation Transport would run them from Aytoun Street and Piccadilly. The bus got filled till it was standing room only and the next one was brought forward. It was smoking on the top deck and no smoking on the bottom deck. Such was the concentration of smokers upstairs that supporters can recall the conductor coming downstairs, eyes watering and 'coughing his lungs out'. These archive pictures are from 1960.

Today, Aytoun Street remains an important part of the city's transportation hub as the Metrolink trams which run along it connect Piccadilly Gardens and Piccadilly Station with the Altrincham line servicing Old Trafford. The street itself is likely to see more students than football supporters, being the home of Manchester Metropolitan University's business school. Not surprisingly, there is no smoking on the Metrolink.

BUSES ON WARWICK ROAD

MATCH SPECIAL

This 1960 photograph (above) shows buses lining up in Warwick Road, ready for the masses to leave Old Trafford at the conclusion of another 90 minutes of football. The picture to the left shows the Match Special's predecessor from 1938, when the tram service took fans back to Albert Square in the heart of Manchester. Trams were gradually phased out during the Forties as the rolling stock was not replaced and spare parts became scarce. They were replaced by trolleybuses and then by diesel coaches and buses. The final tramway abandonment came with the replacement of the Stockport trams on 9 January 1949 and Manchester Corporation Transport was merged with several other operators in 1969.

TODAY

The same spot as it looks today. Traffic along the road is prohibited before and after any events at the Old Trafford football stadium. Current time restrictions, which came into effect in December 2008, begin three hours prior to the match and end two hours afterwards. An efficient tram/Metrolink offers a service every 12 minutes each day of the week, while nearby Old Trafford cricket ground offers car parking in the winter months. The best way to get to Old Trafford is by train; the stadium has its own railway station next to the ground located immediately outside the away end. It was opened in 1857 and renamed from Warwick Road in 1931. The average of 2,000 passenger journeys per day can rise to 9,500 on a match day.

Warwick Road, or Sir Matt Busby Way as it has been known since 1993, connects two of the city's three major sporting venues – Old Trafford football ground at the north end and Old Trafford cricket ground, home of Lancashire county cricket club since 1857, at the south. Bowlers at Lancashire CCC would start their run-up from 'the Warwick Road end'. As with United, LCCC have renamed their section of the road to honour an icon, in this case England fast bowler Brian Statham; a short connecting strip between them retains the Warwick Road name.

AWAY FROM THE PITCH

TOP STRIKERS: CHARLTON AND BEST

In the photograph on the left, Bobby Charlton, watched by Shay Brennan, Bill Foulkes and Jimmy Nicholson, tests out the new bowling alley at the Top Rank Bowl in Manchester, September 1961. In the days before double training sessions and dietary regimes, the players at Manchester United were pretty much left to their own devices once training was over, although this shot was clearly contrived for publicity purposes.

To the right, George Best goes for a strike at the same venue four years later. While the married players would invariably head home, bachelors like Best looked for other ways to pass the time. As long as they did not undertake anything too dangerous or bring the club's name into disrepute, anything that passed a few hours was considered acceptable.

GOLF AND SNOOKER

Having trained in the morning, some United players liked to spend their afternoons at a racecourse or betting shop, after these were legalised in 1961. For others it was snooker, billiards and subsequently pool. As with most clubs, Manchester United had a healthy golf society, with the players regularly out as fours and pairs. At Old Trafford it was invariably Bobby Charlton and Brian Kidd who stood out as the better golf players, with Bobby even having to relinquish his amateur player status in 2004 when he hit a hole in one. With this feat came a prize of a Mercedes car which, under the strict Royal & Ancient Golf Club rules, exceeded the £500 limit for prizes. This left Sir Bobby facing the prospect of having to play off scratch for two years before becoming a professional!

Golf is still the preferred pastime for many of today's players, while at least one Premiership player has his own bowling lane at home.

▶ TODAY

The site of the bowling alley today in Great Stone Road, Stretford. The building became the Hard Rock concert venue after the bowling alley closed. It has now been replaced by a B&Q store, a 10-minute walk from Old Trafford.

THE MIDLAND HOTEL

▲ VENUE OF CHOICE

Built between 1898 and 1903, the iconic 312-bedroom hotel known as the Midland was built by the Midland Railway to serve the adjacent Manchester Central station. It would later find fame as the venue where Charles Stewart Rolls and Frederick Henry Royce met to form Rolls-Royce Limited in 1906. It was also supposedly the venue that Adolf Hitler intended to set up as his headquarters had he succeeded in conquering Britain in World War II.

Promotion back into the top flight at the end of the 1937-38 season called for a celebration at the Midland Hotel, above. Although the margin of their success was as slim as it could be, securing second place ahead of Sheffield United only on goal average.

◄ SUCCESS IN '57

Pictured left at the Midland Hotel, Billy Whelan, Wilf McGuinness, Tommy Taylor (on the saxophone), David Pegg and Bobby Charlton celebrate United's victory over Birmingham City in the FA Cup Semi-Final at Hillsborough in 1957. Now only Aston Villa stood between league leaders Manchester United and the first domestic double of the 20th century. As it happened, United didn't achieve the double until 1994, but arguably would have, had it not been for the injury to Ray Wood.

▶ SIR MATT BECOMES A FREEMAN

Manchester United trio (from left to right), Pat Crerand, Denis Law, Alex Stepney and partners, at the occasion to mark manager Matt Busby's award of Honorary Freeman of the City of Manchester on 23 November 1967.

▲ NOT ALWAYS CELEBRATING

The Midland Hotel has enjoyed its status as the location for countless United celebrations over the years, hosting league championships and cup wins throughout the 20th century. But not just celebrations, for the Midland Hotel has also hosted numerous dinners in its French Room for visiting teams in both European competition and friendlies throughout the Fifties.

The hotel retained its connection with Manchester United as the century came to a close. The French Room is reputedly where David Beckham and the then Victoria Adams enjoyed their first date. On a not so celebratory note, Sir Alex Ferguson is familiar with the hotel as the venue for FA disciplinary hearings.

WAGS AND GLAMOUR AT UNITED

◄ BOBBY AND BRIDE

Bobby Charlton and his bride, the former Norma Ball, are pictured about to depart on their honeymoon after their wedding at Middleton Junction in Manchester in 1961. The event would have been a low-key affair by comparison with today, with no thought of exclusive picture deals with the glossy magazines of the day, although the status enjoyed by Bobby was sufficient to bring out a healthy local crowd to the event.

The wives of the Manchester United players of the Fifties and Sixties were completely different from their present-day counterparts. Then they were most likely to be local girls, someone the player had met at a relatively young age and matured with together. If they worked it was invariably office jobs – Norma Ball worked for a Manchester fashion agency and met Bobby Charlton at a local ice rink. Many would give up working in order to raise their families, especially with their men absent so often on football duties. Today's wives will often have their own career paths they have followed prior to becoming married to a professional footballer, with many coming from the world of modelling. There is still the occasional player who will buck the trend – Michael Carrick met Lisa Roughead at high school in Tyne and Wear and married her after going out for 13 years.

◄ UP FOR THE CUP

Players' wives – from left to right, Mrs June Brennan, Mrs Norma Charlton, Mrs Jeanette Quixall, Mrs Joan Herd, Miss Noreen Ferry (Pat Crerand's fiancée), Mrs Diana Law, Mrs Pat Setters and Mrs Ann Dunne – arrive at St Pancras Station on route to the FA Cup Final at Wembley in 1963. While the players had been safely ensconced in their London hotel for much of the week preparing for the Final against Leicester City, their wives travelled down to London on the day of the game and would not meet up with their husbands until after the match, which Manchester United would win 3-1.

▲ THE UNITED-ETTES

American-style cheerleaders were tried at Old Trafford in October 1963. The Manchester United-ettes didn't catch on as a form of pre-match entertainment, and neither did the beauty pageant Miss Manchester United run by the club in the Eighties.

TODAY

Daniela Martins is the Portuguese girlfriend of United winger Luis Nani. She moved from Lisbon to a London council house when she was eight years old after her dad got a job as a bus driver in the capital. She met Nani on a holiday back to Lisbon in 2007. She conforms to the WAG stereotype in being a model and having finished runner-up in Miss América Latina 2004, but she also has four A-levels and a degree in journalism to prove there are brains behind the pretty face. Unlike many fellow WAGs she says she still shops in Primark and IKEA. As of 2011, she and Nani have been together for four years.

BOBBY CHARLTON: A CAREER IN PICTURES

CAREER DETAILS: Bobby Charlton held the record number of United appearances with 758 until Ryan Giggs surpassed him in 2008. During his 17-year spell as a first-team player at Old Trafford he notched an unrivalled 249 goals, a record he still holds.

Born near Newcastle upon Tyne in 1937, the long-striding Charlton joined the Old Trafford ground staff in June 1953 and made his full United debut in October 1956, scoring twice. By the end of 1956-57 he had helped the Babes to Championship success, contributing 10 goals. He also scored in the FA Cup Semi-Final, going on to play Aston Villa in the Final. A survivor of the Munich crash of February 1958, he returned to action the following month and made his full international debut in April against Scotland. He won 106 caps, scoring 49 goals.

◄ **OUR BOBBY**

Elizabeth (better known as Cissie) Charlton playing football with her sons Gordon (10), Bobby (15) and Tommy (7) outside their home in Ashington. Cissie came from a football dynasty as all four of her brothers played professional football (as had her father Jack, who played for Ashington during their brief Football League career) and her cousin was 'Wor' Jackie Milburn. Not pictured enjoying the street kickabout is Cissie's eldest son Jack who was already on the books of Leeds United at the time this picture was taken. Between them, the Milburn and Charlton clans would amass 154 international caps and 14 winners' medals in major competitions.

▲ ASHINGTON RECOVERY

Less than two weeks after surviving the Munich air crash, Bobby Charlton returned to his family home in Beatrice Street in Ashington. Proof that he was well on the road to a full recovery can be seen here, as he enjoys a kickabout in the backyard with several young fans.

▲ HOSTILE RECEPTION

Bobby Charlton leads the Manchester United players out for training at the Army Stadium in Belgrade the day before their European Cup Quarter-Final second leg clash against Red Star in 1958. United held a slender 2-1 lead after the first leg in Manchester and knew Red Star would be difficult opponents – United had to come from behind in the first leg before securing their victory at Old Trafford. In Belgrade it was a different story; two first half goals from Charlton helped put them 0-3 up at half time.

▶ ENGLAND'S FUTURE

Bobby Charlton on the cover of *World Sports* six months after the Munich disaster. Following England's poor showing at the 1958 World Cup in Sweden, there were growing calls for the England side to be built around the likes of Charlton, who had appeared in several of England's warm-up matches (including a scoring appearance in the match against Scotland in April 1958, two months after Munich) but had been omitted from the squad for the Finals.

CAREER DETAILS: In 1964 Charlton moved from left-wing to midfield where he was able to be more involved, and this contributed greatly to United's Championship win that year. He was equally instrumental in helping England to World Cup victory in 1966, after which he pulled off the hat-trick of Footballer of the Year, European Footballer of the Year and the referees' Model Player. The pinnacle of his career came in 1968 when Charlton helped United to their European Cup win over Benfica at Wembley.

Bobby Charlton retired at the end of the 1972-73 season and, having already been awarded an OBE, was upgraded to CBE in January 1974. He was knighted in 1994, and remains a proud United director today.

◄ FAMILY LIFE

A rare 'at home' picture from 1964. Bobby Charlton washes and polishes his car outside his home in Urmston, Manchester, watched by his wife Norma and baby daughter Suzanne (who would later become a BBC weather forecaster). Sadly for Bobby this is all he would be polishing at the end of the season – despite pushing Liverpool all the way in the league championship, United had to settle for second place at the end of the campaign.

▲ SIXTH LEAGUE TITLE

Bobby Charlton pictured in November 1964 at Highbury ahead of league leaders Manchester United's match against Arsenal. While Arsenal languished in mid-table, United had registered twelve victories and four draws from their opening 18 matches and led the league by a point from Chelsea. At the end of the match United would have a further two points thanks to a 3-2 victory and at the end of the season their sixth league title, beating Leeds United on goal difference.

▶ BEATING REAL MADRID

Jimmy Murphy (assistant manager), Bobby Charlton and Matt Busby (manager) celebrate in May 1968 after Manchester United's 3-3 draw with Real Madrid; enough to give them passage into the European Cup Final. Holding a 1-0 lead from the first leg at Old Trafford, United seemed to wilt during the first half of the return leg, falling 3-1 behind at half time in front of 120,000 passionate Real Madrid supporters. Throwing caution to the wind in the second half, United were rewarded by goals from David Sadler and Bill Foulkes in five minutes to achieve a place in the Final, which would take place at Wembley in two weeks' time.

▲ EUROPEAN FOOTBALLER OF THE YEAR

Matt Busby congratulates Bobby Charlton on winning the 1966 Ballon d'Or, or more commonly known as the European Footballer of the Year award, which was presented at Old Trafford by Max Urbini of *France Football*. Instigated in 1956, the award had been won by United team-mate Denis Law in 1964. While United had ended 1966 without a trophy, it was still an exceptional year for Charlton, who won the FWA Footballer of the Year as well as the European award and helped England win the World Cup. It was his performances in the World Cup that enabled Bobby to finish ahead of Benfica and Portugal's Eusébio, and Bayern Munich and West Germany's Franz Beckenbauer in the race for the Ballon d'Or.

BOBBY CHARLTON: END OF AN ERA

THE LAST 'BABE' HANGS UP HIS BOOTS

After 17 years and a total of 758 appearances for the Manchester United first team, Charlton called time on his playing career after United's 1-0 defeat at Stamford Bridge in April 1973. After the highs of four league titles, an FA Cup winners' medal and a European Cup winners' medal, a final finish of 18th was hardly the way Bobby would have liked to finish his United career. However, after becoming manager at Deepdale with Preston North End the following season, installing former United team-mate Nobby Stiles as player-coach, Bobby came out of retirement and made 38 league appearances in an attempt to coax Preston back up the league after their relegation to the Third Division at the end of his first season in charge. After leaving

Preston and deciding management was not for him, Bobby would make further appearances for Waterford, Arcadia Shepherds, Bangor City, Newcastle KB United and Blacktown City before hanging up his boots for good in 1980. In the photo above Charlton shoots for goal in the league clash with West Ham United at Old Trafford in August 1970. With Manchester United still looking for their first home win of the season and West Ham having drawn their opening three games, a draw was always on the cards, with John Fitzpatrick scoring for Manchester United in the 1-1 stalemate. Despite Charlton's effort, the West Ham defenders, including Martin Peters, Trevor Brooking and Billy Bonds, repelled this particular effort.

▼ 1970 SEASON

Bobby Charlton contemplates the new season, the second with manager Wilf McGuinness in charge at Old Trafford. United had finished the 1969-70 season in eighth place in the table, a whopping 21 points behind champions Everton, and hopes were high that United could return to their former glories. Unfortunately 1970-71 would prove to be another disappointment, with the club's directors calling time on McGuinness's time in charge in December and United finishing the season in the same eighth place.

▼ FINAL FAREWELL

Chelsea chairman Joe Mears presented Bobby Charlton with an engraved cigarette case ahead of his 606th and final league appearance for Manchester United, shortly before the league clash between the two sides at Stamford Bridge in April 1973. Also in attendance for the presentation was Bobby's manager for much of his career at Old Trafford, Sir Matt Busby, sporting uncharacteristic glasses.

SUPPORTER POWER

1926

A section of the crowd at Bramall Lane, Sheffield for the FA Cup Semi-Final clash between the two Manchester rivals, City and United in March 1926. The second ever cup meeting between the two sides saw City march into the Final with a 3-0 victory.

Five years later, United were attracting crowds of less than 4,000 for some games and were relegated after finishing bottom of Division One. An early dose of supporter power was to be seen in October 1930 when 3,000 fans met to try and stage an eventually unsuccessful boycott of the match against Arsenal. On 18 December 1931 the club was refused more credit and the players could not be paid. With debts mounting, secretary-manager Walter Crickmer turned to benefactor James W. Gibson whose gift of £2,000 kept the wolves at bay. Mr Gibson proposed a new issue of 'Patrons' Tickets' – an early form of season ticket – hoping to raise funds. The response was disappointing, but he decided to pledge more of his own funds and change the club's fortunes.

▲ 2010

Today's supporters are unafraid to show their feelings, as these 'Glazer Out' banners from 2010 show. The protest against the American family that bought control of United in 2005 reflects the unease at the debt the club was subsequently saddled with, a figure that had reached £716.5 million by 2010. The green and gold colours of Newton Heath were adopted as an emblem, while other disillusioned supporters deserted Old Trafford completely and backed the formation of non-league club FC United of Manchester. The campaign was effective enough for the club to take the rare step of making some 4,000 season tickets openly available in an effort to match the previous season's total sale of 54,000.

▶ SUPPORT FROM DAVID BECKHAM

Former United legend David Beckham, returning to Old Trafford for the first time in March 2010 as an AC Milan player, picks up a scarf in the colours of Newton Heath on leaving the pitch. The game was also the first time a member of the Glazer family, Avram, had attended a home game since the announcement of the £500m bond issue in January that would help alleviate the club's debt. Expressions of supporter unrest perhaps understandably diminished as United powered towards their 19th title and reached the Champions League Final in 2011.

AUTOGRAPH HUNTERS

◄ JOHN CONNELLY

United winger John Connelly runs the gauntlet of autograph hunters as he arrives at Old Trafford for training. He stayed at Old Trafford for just over two seasons after signing from Burnley, making 113 appearances and scoring 35 goals. He was a fringe member of the England squad which won the World Cup in 1966, playing just one game, and was shortly afterwards transferred to Blackburn Rovers.

▼ GEORGE BEST

George Best signs an autograph on the forecourt of Old Trafford shortly before boarding the coach in January 1970. Best was the first football superstar. While players in the Fifties had been content to supplement their meagre football income with advertising assignments for cigarettes, Brylcreem and Bovril, George Best took the concept many stages further, modelling menswear before launching his own boutique.

▲ NO AUTOGRAPHS

A reminder to George Best, along with all other Manchester United players, not to sign autographs on the field of play. The message, which hangs at the club's training facility at The Cliff, was also repeated in just about every programme but did little to deter schoolboys flocking onto the pitch at the final whistle. While Best soon became used to the adulation of the fans in Manchester, he found it slightly incomprehensible on his return visits to Belfast and admitted that he still considered himself 'wee Georgie from the Cregagh Estate' and felt detached from the headlines and news stories that regularly appeared in the local paper.

▼ TODAY

Dimitar Berbatov, United's top scorer in the 2010-11 season (including five against Blackburn), signs an autograph for a fan wearing a replica of his shirt. Access to players in the 21st century is usually restricted to their emergence from the Carrington training complex, but they remain fair game at public events.

▲ DUNCAN EDWARDS

One of the last autographs Duncan Edwards would ever give, signing his name on the pitch at Highbury in February 1958, five minutes before Manchester United's match with Arsenal. After a 5-4 victory for United, the team were heading off to Belgrade for the second leg of their European Cup Quarter-Final, which would ultimately lead to the Munich air crash. Of all United's players past and present, Duncan Edwards' remains the most collectable of autographs, with examples of his signature in programmes, autograph books and magazines regularly turning up on both online and auction house sales. Of particular value are Manchester United or England items that are additionally signed by Tommy Taylor and Roger Byrne, who also died at Munich.

GEORGE BEST:
A CAREER IN PICTURES

CAREER DETAILS: At the age of 15, Best was discovered in Belfast by United scout Bob Bishop, who famously sent United manager Matt Busby a telegram that simply read 'I think I've found you a genius'. George Best took time to settle in both Manchester as a city and United as a team. After running back home because he was homesick, George was eventually sent to digs at Mrs Fullaway's home in Chorlton-cum-Hardy. At the time he arrived at the club he was too young to sign with the club officially, so United found him a job working at the Manchester Canal as a tea boy during the day and training with the amateurs two nights a week. Unsuited for this and a subsequent job in a timber yard (he lasted just half a day), George was signed as a full-time ground staff boy, even though this was technically illegal.

By May 1963 he had been upgraded to the professional ranks on £17 a week and made his first-team debut against West Bromwich Albion at Old Trafford and helped United to a 1-0 victory. Two months later, in just his second first-team game came the first of his 137 league goals for the club, netting in United's 5-1 victory over Burnley on 28 December. Two days earlier, without Best, United had been thumped 6-1 at Turf Moor!

By 1964 George was almost a regular in the side and would end the season with 26 appearances and six goals to his credit as United finished league runners-up to Liverpool. The following season United claimed their first league title since the Busby Babes era, with George missing just one match all season. His tally of 10 goals also proved crucial as Manchester United beat Leeds United by goal average in the final reckoning. He also helped United reach the Semi-Finals of the Inter Cities Fairs Cup (beaten in a play-off by Juventus), the Semi-Finals of the FA Cup (beaten by Leeds United after a replay) and made the first of his 37 appearances for Northern Ireland to cap a memorable first full season.

▲ TEENAGE KICKS

Away from the pressures of football, George would often relax in his room at Mrs Fullaway's council house listening to the latest releases on the record player. Best also found other ways to relax that allowed him to socialise with his two closest friends – David Sadler and John Fitzpatrick – that involved a few beers. The alcohol helped the shy youngster to relax and had the added bonus of reducing his inhibitions when it came to dealings with attractive women.

▶ STOP THE PRESS JOB

By November 1964, George was not only a regular in the first team but an integral part of the side that was on its way to their sixth league title. By this time, it was apparent that Best would make the grade as a professional footballer so his father felt confident enough in his son's footballing ability to inform the local printer, with whom he had lined up 'back-up' employment, that the offer of a job would no longer be required. Today's opponents Arsenal were brushed aside 3-2 at Highbury.

▼ IN TROUBLE?

A thoughtful George Best on the physio's bench at United's training ground, the Cliff, 1965. The team would also train at Old Trafford on a Friday morning and the players dreaded being called into the referee's room that Matt Busby used as his temporary office. Best was called in to see the manager during the 1965-66 season to be told he was being dropped and needed to improve his performances. Busby had witnessed many players ruin their career through drink and wanted to shock Best into a more acceptable social life that didn't include partying until the early hours.

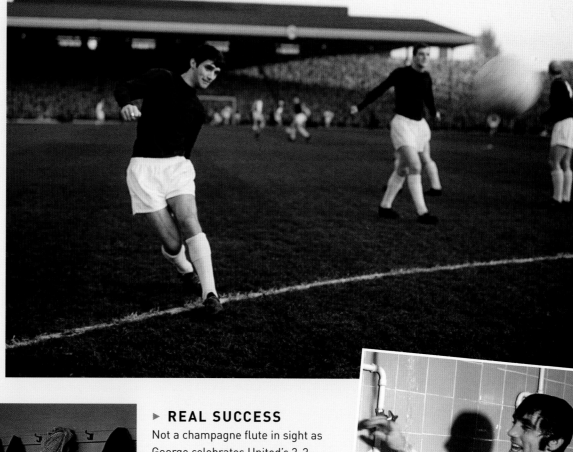

▶ REAL SUCCESS

Not a champagne flute in sight as George celebrates United's 3-3 draw against Real Madrid at the Bernabeu Stadium in May 1968 that takes them into the European Cup Final. Matt Busby proved himself a tactical mastermind and buoyed his disappointed players in the half-time team talk, pointing out that they were still in the game despite being 3-1 down. He switched David Sadler to a more attacking role, a move that paid dividends when Sadler scored to bring United back into the game.

CAREER DETAILS: The Portuguese media can take much of the credit for bestowing superstar status on George Best; after a European Cup Quarter-Final against Benfica in Lisbon in which he scored twice and created three more in United's 5-1 victory, he was hailed as 'O Quinto Beatle' – the fifth Beatle. With his long hair, good looks and growing celebrity lifestyle, it was a status he took to comfortably. Fortunately, at least as far as the next two or three years were concerned, he maintained the headlines on the back pages for his prowess on the field as he helped United win the league title in 1967 and the European Cup the following year, also winning the European Player of the Year and the FWA Player of the Year awards the same year.

That was as good as it got for George Best and by association Manchester United; growing outside influences, the eventual retirement of Matt Busby and, as George himself would later state, United's inability to strengthen an ageing side saw George make the headlines on the front page for all the wrong reasons as one decade came to a close and another was ushered in. Indeed, while he is rightly regarded as one of the finest players ever to wear the red shirt of United, he was at the peak of his powers for less than 10 years.

▲ BEST AGAINST CITY

Familiar territory for George; racing away with the ball with an opposing player trailing in his wake, in this case Colin Bell of local rivals Manchester City at Maine Road. Despite the fact that there have been more than 200 derby matches between the two Manchester clubs during their long and illustrious histories, George Best only managed to score against City on three occasions. His first successful strike came in his fourth out of 15 appearances in the fixture, a 3-1 defeat at Old Trafford in which Best opened the scoring only for his side to concede three times as their opponents powered towards the First Division title. Best scored twice in May 1971 as United ran out 4-3 winners in Matt Busby's final competitive game in charge of the club.

► SUPPORT NEEDED

Training away from the limelight and without the screams of the crowds, George Best does what he does best out on the training field in 1965. Best felt somewhat let down by the lack of assistance offered by United when it came to his extra-curricular problems. He was of the belief that, as he was performing for the club on the pitch, they should have tried more to curb his lifestyle off it and described Matt Busby as more of a headmaster than a father figure.

▼ FOOTBALLER OF THE YEAR

France Football's Editor-In-Chief Max Urbini makes his bi-annual pilgrimage to Old Trafford to present the European Player of the Year award, this time to George Best in 1968.

► 'MARADONA GOOD, PELÉ BETTER, GEORGE BEST'

Five days after Best's death from multiple organ failure, the Old Trafford crowd pay their respects by holding aloft posters of their favourite son. In spite of the fact that it had been more than 30 years since his last game for United, the fans always appreciated his talent and mourned the passing of a legend. Fittingly, the opponents at Old Trafford were West Bromwich Albion in the Carling (League) Cup, the same opposition that had seen George make his debut in a United first-team shirt. That had been a 1-0 home win; in November 2005 United won 3-1.

GEORGE BEST: DIGS, CHORLTON

LODGING WITH MRS FULLAWAY

George's homesickness was so bad that, when originally invited to trial for United in July 1961 with friend Eric McMordie, the pair returned to Belfast after a single night. Matt Busby persuaded him back to Manchester, while McMordie eventually signed for Middlesbrough three years later.

The solution was to lodge George with Mary Fullaway at her council house at 9 Aycliffe Avenue, Chorlton-cum-Hardy. His landlady's house was situated near to Matt Busby's, which the young Belfast lad found, to put it mildly, intimidating. Best would try to hide if he saw the manager's car driving down the road in an attempt to avoid being offered a lift. On the rare occasion that he failed, he found himself tongue-tied in the presence of a United legend. Mrs Fullaway did her utmost to beef Best up but results were not forthcoming straight away as he found his footballing career limited to the B team.

Best became a friend of Mary Fullaway's teenage son Steve until, perhaps inevitably, they fell out after George took a fancy to his girlfriend. A 2009 TV drama *Best: His Mother's Son*, included references to the pair's relationship. Although he moved out to an architect-designed house in Bramhall, when things got on top of him in 1975, he actually moved back in with the Fullaways.

◄ TODAY

The world's paparazzi no longer camp out in Aycliffe Avenue. In 1969 George moved to a £30,000 house in Bramhall; his only stipulations were that it had a sunken bath and a snooker room. It was the start of the move by wealthy United players to seek privacy in the leafy commuter belt of Bramhall, Prestbury and Alderley Edge. Cheshire resident Rio Ferdinand spent £5 million on a new house with seven bedrooms, an indoor pool and fitness centre, while Michael Carrick bulldozed the existing house on the land to build a dream £4.25 million family home with seven bedrooms, a library, cinema, wine cellar, indoor pool, private gym and patio with hot-tub.

GEORGE BEST: STAFF

THE FIRST FOOTBALL SUPERSTAR

Left and opposite: George Best, his driver Bill White, secretary Pearl Goodman and business manager Malcolm Mooney pictured in Trafford Park, not far from one of the United player's first jobs at the Manchester Ship Canal. Best helped usher in the new era when football stars needed 'staff' to cope with the pressures of the job (and also driving bans).

The abolition of the maximum wage had changed English football forever. Johnny Haynes may well have become the first player to be paid £100 a week, but George Best was keen to see his wages at £1,000 a week, less than a decade after Haynes' pay packet had reached that first plateau. That was just George's earnings from Manchester United; there were further riches to be earned from a wide variety of sources.

Prior to 1966 the only manager George needed to worry about was Matt Busby, his manager at Manchester United, but with the moniker 'El Beatle' came the opportunity to branch out and earn money, serious money too, from a wide variety of sources. All of this needed managing, so Ken Stanley was appointed manager (he was also Denis Law's agent), handling the day-to-day requests for interviews and other business propositions. Malcolm Mooney was given the title business manager and would eventually end up running Best's boutiques before his untimely death in a car crash. Pearl Goodman was appointed secretary, which basically meant keeping his diary up to date, dealing with the day-to-day correspondence and ensuring George turned up at the right place at the right time.

Aside from his shop interests, George Best's name was used for a wide variety of products, including most famously Cookstown Sausages, with the television commercial including the phrase 'the Best family sausages' and modelling assignments for Great Universal Stores.

However, since it was football that had made George's name and reputation, there were countless football-related items bearing his name. A deal with book publishers Pelham produced five editions of the *George Best Soccer Annual*, usually with an introduction by Ken Stanley, an autobiography entitled *Best of Both Worlds* in 1968 and an instructional book *On the Ball* in which George showed how you could learn from the great players. With regards to commercial exploitation, later players undoubtedly learnt from George Best.

▲ MALCOLM MOONEY

The man in the passenger seat of the Iso Rivolta sportscar George is trying out in 1969 is his business manager Malcolm Mooney. Mooney was a Mancunian entrepreneur with experience in the rag trade and helped George open his first boutique in Sale when Best was just 19. He went on to open the well-known Belle Epoque restaurant in Knutsford before his life was cut short in a car accident.

▶ TODAY

The surrounding industrial area of Old Trafford has changed profoundly in a generation and the warehouses and factories of the Sixties have gone, while up the road, redevelopment of the area around the Ship Canal has seen the birth of Salford Quays and the arrival of the Lowry art gallery and theatres.

BELFAST BOY

Country and Western singer Don Fardon poses with George Best and sandwich man Mike Hawkin outside the George Best Rogue clothes store on Market Street, Manchester, in March 1970. Fardon was about to release his tribute to Best entitled 'Belfast Boy' which had been used as the theme tune to a George Best TV documentary. It spent five weeks on the charts between April and May 1970 and reached No.32. The track was re-issued in 2006 after Best's death.

TODAY

The Edwardia boutique has had many occupants since Best left Manchester and today hosts a branch of Starbucks.

GEORGE BEST SHOPS

CASHING IN

In 1966, George Best opened his first boutique in Cross Street, Sale, the main road running through the town. Then part of Cheshire, Sale lies five miles south of Manchester city centre.

In 1967, he added a second, larger store in Bridge Street, Manchester, an upmarket area just round the corner from the prestigious Kendal Milne department store. The shop interior was designed by architect Frazer Crane who also designed Best's Bramhall house. The Manchester store pictured left and above traded under the name Edwardia, reflecting the Edwardian influence on Sixties British pop culture.

One of George's partners in the venture was his great friend, Manchester City winger Mike Summerbee (above). Many of Best's female fans waited outside Edwardia hoping for a glimpse of their idol but they were likely to be disappointed. Although the two players posed in and around the shop for publicity photographs, they had little to do with the day-to-day running of the business, which was left to a third partner, Malcolm Mooney.

Best also had a stake in two Manchester nightclubs, Slack Alice's on Bootle Street just off Deansgate and Oscars, off Princess Street near Chinatown.

ANY OTHER BUSINESS?

◄ FROM A CATERING FAMILY

Scot Lou Macari's Italian immigrant grandparents ran a successful café in Largs, Ayrshire, while his father also worked in the catering industry. After his father's premature death Macari decided to bring his mother down to Manchester, and in 1978 invested in a chip shop near Old Trafford for her to run. But this coincided with Macari's involvement in the World Cup and she died before he could organise her move south. The shop proved a success nonetheless and a visit became a matchday ritual for many fans.

▼ LOU MACARI

Diminutive striker Luigi 'Lou' Macari, born in 1949, was already a Scottish international when he moved south from Celtic in 1973 for a fee of £200,000. He had scored 57 goals in 100 appearances in green and white, a strike rate that had led to competition for his services. United's Pat Crerand, also ex-Celtic, successfully persuaded him to talk to United, having encountered him at a Liverpool game Macari attended as manager Bill Shankly's guest.

Though he joined a failing team that would be relegated under Tommy Docherty, Macari's 11 goals helped United win the Second Division title in 1975 and he would stick around to play 400 games for the Red Devils.

As the goals dried up towards the end of the Seventies, Macari was moved into a midfield role by Docherty and this gave him a new lease of life. But incoming boss Ron Atkinson benched him for his last two seasons before he left Old Trafford in 1984 to become Swindon player-manager.

▲ SUPERSTAR SHOE REPAIRER

Denis Law signs autographs in March 1964 outside his shoe repair shop in Moston Lane, Blackley (pronounced Blake-ly), some three miles to the north of Manchester. United legends Wilf McGuinness and Roger Byrne hailed from the town.

While today's players are able to earn enough to keep them for life, the United legends of the past had to make a living after hanging up their boots. Scots forward David Herd, a United player from 1961-68, founded David Herd Limited, a successful used car dealer based in the Manchester suburb of Flixton and stocking a wide range of second-hand cars. It still operates today though Herd himself has retired. Fellow Sixties legend Tony Dunne runs a driving range in Altrincham, while his fellow European Cup winner David Sadler became a manager for a building society in Hale, Greater Manchester.

▲ TODAY

The Lou Macari Fish & Chip Shop at 684 Chester Road is still owned by the former United legend over 30 years after he opened it. It is so popular with match-goers it even has its own page on the social networking site Facebook. However, fans hoping to get a glimpse of Lou taking a turn behind the deep fat fryers are about as likely to see him as Best's teenage fans were of seeing their idol in Rogue or Edwardia. Lou, who lives in Stoke-on-Trent, still maintains an active association with the club, and is currently a pundit with United's MUTV television channel.

DENIS LAW: A CAREER IN PICTURES

CAREER DETAILS: Quicksilver Scots forward Law scored an incredible 237 goals during his 11 years with United, helping the club to two league titles, one FA Cup and the European Cup, though he missed the Final through injury. An aggressive streak that got him into trouble with referees was matched by a knack for being in the right place at the right time and speed off the mark.

Born in 1940, he signed with Huddersfield as an apprentice at 15, an operation on a squint giving blurred sight only to his right eye. Matt Busby spotted Law in an FA Youth Cup tie against United and offered Huddersfield £10,000. This was rejected and he made his league debut aged 16. Busby, then manager of Scotland, capped him against Wales in 1958 and he scored in a 3-0 win.

◄ HOMESICK SCOT

Six years later than he intended and at the third attempt, Manchester United manager Matt Busby finally landed his man. Pictured in July 1962, Denis puts pen to paper surrounded by Italian agent Gigi Peronace, Matt Busby, United assistant manager Jimmy Murphy and club secretary Les Olive.

In 1960 Manchester City had outbid Busby with an offer of £55,000 and secured his signature. The following year, with the maximum wage in England still in place, Denis joined the ranks of those turned by the promise of rich rewards on offer in Italy (along with Jimmy Greaves and Gerry Hitchens) and joined Torino for £110,000, a then record fee.

Like Jimmy Greaves, Law was unable to settle in Italy, at odds with both the defensive nature of the game and the strict regime that controlled the players. The final straw came after being sent off against Napoli, which resulted in Denis putting in a transfer request. Matt Busby rescued him from Italy and paid a new transfer record of £115,000 to bring him back to Manchester.

Denis Law controls a high ball during Manchester United's league clash with Newcastle United at Old Trafford in September 1968. He is being watched by Newcastle defender Ollie Burton. Law scored once in his side's 3–1 victory.

► **EUROPEAN FOOTBALLER OF THE YEAR**

Bobby Charlton described Law as 'easily the best inside-forward in Britain,' adding 'When he's really in form, he's virtually unstoppable.' And the European footballing media noticed, too.

Duncan Edwards had come joint third in the voting in 1957 but Denis Law was United's first recipient of the European Footballer of the Year award. He is shown here receiving the award in 1964. He was followed by Bobby Charlton two years later and George Best two years after that (with Charlton finishing runner-up to Best). It would take until 2008 for another United player to win the prestigious award. Eric Cantona, David Beckham and Cristiano Ronaldo made the top three in 1993, 1999 and 2007 respectively but Ronaldo finally won it in 2008.

As a postscript, in Holland in May 1969, a newly born child was named after his father's footballing idol. The authorities, however, insisted on a double 'n' to avoid confusion with Denise... so Dennis Bergkamp it was.

CAREER DETAILS: After short spells for Huddersfield, Manchester City and Torino, Law arrived at United in 1962 for a British record fee of £115,000. He earned many domestic and international honours during the Sixties – Law played for Scotland 55 times and is their all-time joint top goalscorer with 30 – while his United strike rate was better than a goal every two games. Incoming manager Tommy Docherty gave him a free transfer at the end of the 1972-73 season, and he returned to Manchester City to score a goal against United on the day he learned that they were relegated to the Second Division in 1974. He retired from football at 34 in 1974 and has since preferred punditry to an active role in the game.

▶ BACK TO BELGRADE

Captain for the day, Denis Law leads the Manchester United players out on to the field for the European Cup Semi-Final against Partizan Belgrade in April 1966. Close behind are David Herd, Harry Gregg and Bobby Charlton. United eventually lost 2-0 with both goals coming in the second half.

▶ LAW'S RECORD

Denis Law at his free-flowing best, evading a tackle by West Ham United's (and England's) Bobby Moore in a game against the Hammers from 1970. Denis Law holds many United goalscoring records, including the most goals in a season (46 in 1963-64) and the most hat-tricks (18). He is also the second highest United goalscorer of all time, with 237 from 404 appearances, a higher goalscoring ratio than either Best or Charlton. Law would also have been the 20th century's top FA Cup goalscorer (instead of Ian Rush) had six goals in an abandoned 1961 tie not been expunged.

▼ PROFILE PICTURE

Denis Law was immediately accepted at Old Trafford despite his brief City past, remarking 'I didn't get any hassle when I switched clubs.' He is an admirer of Carlos Tevez, a similarly quicksilver performer, who moved in the opposite direction in 2009 and who endured vilification from Reds fans. Law believed it was 'a wee bit different if you are foreign. It may make it harder.' He, of course, made his first move via Italy.

▲ RATED BY FERGUSON

In 2009, United manager and fellow Scot Sir Alex Ferguson named Law, now a TV and press pundit, as the man he most admired as a player. The same year Ferguson dressed up as a chef in a prank to catch out Law on United's dedicated television channel, MUTV.

It is often thought that Law's winning goal for City against United in 1974 relegated his former club, but it turned out they would have gone down even had the match been drawn. Law walked off the pitch with head bowed when he was substituted immediately afterwards. This was his last club game, as he retired after appearing for Scotland in the 1974 World Cup that summer. City were bringing in young blood and Law understandably declined the offer of reserve-team football.

THE UNITED TRINITY

◄ BEST, LAW AND CHARLTON

United's three stars pose with models at Old Trafford showing off a range of (slightly too large) overcoats in May 1967. It was a situation unlikely to phase George Best but less common for Denis Law and certainly for Bobby Charlton. Charlton had differing views of his fellow professionals. He had little time for Best but described Law as, 'Tough as teak; Denis could never be intimidated, no matter how many times a defender kicked him,' while Matt Busby said: 'Signing him was without doubt one of my best ever bits of business.'

Between them, Best, Law and Charlton scored 665 goals for Manchester United and all won the coveted European Footballer of the Year award; Denis Law in 1964, Bobby Charlton in 1966 and George Best in 1968. While Bobby was a United player between 1956 and 1973, Denis between 1962 and 1973 and George between 1963 and 1974, it is the four-year period between 1964 and 1968 that cemented their collective and individual reputations at Old Trafford, culminating in the European Cup Final victory at Wembley against Benfica in 1968. That was also the match that Denis Law was forced to miss owing to injury, although he did score early on in the competition to set United on their way.

While their names appear to be forever entwined, they were all very different characters. Denis and George would often play with short fuses, which usually led to being booked or dismissed during the course of a season. Bobby was much less likely to explode, picking up just two bookings during his entire playing career, once for United (improbably, against Spurs in the 1967 Charity Shield) and once for England. Where they were all explosive was in front of goal; with Bobby scoring more than any other United player, followed by Denis in second place and George in equal fourth with Dennis Viollet.

► FINAL REUNION

The Holy Trinity are pictured together for the last time as George Best, Bobby Charlton and Denis Law receive National Football Awards at Old Trafford in 2000.

▲ STRAINED RELATIONS

Bobby Charlton and George Best at Old Trafford, 1969. At times, the pair were not on speaking terms and Best refused to play in Charlton's testimonial match against Celtic, reportedly saying that 'to do so would be hypocritical'. In return, Charlton 'did not think his lifestyle was compatible with being a professional footballer, though for a while at least I accepted that he was doing extraordinary things.'

▼ TODAY

Shortly after the death of George Best in 2005 the club considered honouring the trio with a statue. Fittingly, it faces a statue of that other iconic figure from Manchester United's history, Sir Matt Busby (also sculptured by Philip Jackson a decade previously), perhaps the ultimate accolade. Certainly both surviving players viewed it as such. 'The sculptor has done a magnificent job and to have a statue erected by the most famous club in the world is a tremendous honour for me' was Denis's take on it, while Bobby said, 'Many great players have come through at Manchester United over the years, so this is one of the greatest things that has ever happened to me.'

The statue was finally unveiled at Old Trafford in May 2008 on the 40th anniversary of that famous European Cup victory. Bobby and Denis were joined by George's sister Barbara McNarry and current United manager Sir Alex Ferguson for the unveiling.

QUICKS OF OLD TRAFFORD

▲ MADE IN MANCHESTER

Pictured in the Twenties, the Ford showroom at Chester Road, Old Trafford was one of the earliest motor car dealerships in the Manchester area. Ford had opened their first European assembly plant in Trafford Park only a year after Manchester United moved to Old Trafford, and the Model T Fords seen on the forecourt of Quicks were built just down the road. Originally known as H&J Quick, the company forged strong links with United, the Old Trafford ground being a short walk away.

▶ GIGGS' FIRST UNITED MOTOR

A fresh-faced 18-year-old Ryan Giggs receives his new car in regulation United red in November 1991. The publicity benefits of such arrangements for 'Quicks of Old Trafford' was clear. Giggs had made his first team debut in March 1991 having been on the United books since 1987. After establishing his place in the side, senior professionals Steve Bruce and Bryan Robson suggested that he should go and ask manager, Sir Alex Ferguson, if he qualified for a club car. The teenage Giggs duly knocked on the manager's door and posed the question. 'He went absolutely nuts,' Giggs recalled. It was only a while later he realised the older players had been winding him up about the car, knowing the reaction he'd get. By November the following season, however, he was clearly valuable enough to take delivery of a Ford Escort.

TODAY

Like Ryan Giggs, the former Quicks showroom at 660 Chester Road, at the junction with Sir Matt Busby Way, is still a familiar feature of the Manchester landscape. It is also still a Ford franchise, though it now goes under the name of Evans Halshaw. Since 2004, Audi have been official car suppliers to Manchester United and in 2011 mounted a stand of cars behind the United Trinity statue, in addition to supplying cars to United figures and having their branding embossed on the Old Trafford dugout seats.

Like Giggs, the red Escort has had a long career. After a year in his possession Giggs sold it to an aspiring Manchester United Youth Team player, one David Beckham. The J-registered 1.3 Escort is featured in the documentary *There's Only One David Beckham* and also gets a mention in his book, *My Side*. It was eventually bought by the *News of the World* and given away in a 1999 competition. The winner, Mrs Rita McGoldrick, ran it happily for 10 years before putting it up for sale on eBay in 2009. It sold for in excess of £15,000.

UNITED PLAYERS AND THEIR CARS

◄ DENIS LAW: FORD CONSUL CAPRI

Denis Law arrives at Old Trafford in July 1962 to sign for United from Torino. His car is a Ford Consul Capri, which had gone on sale for the first time in Britain in January 1962. The earliest version of the Capri offered many features considered unusual at the time, such as four headlights, variable speed wipers, 9.5in front disc brakes and dimming dashboard lights. The four-speed transmission was available with either a column or floor change.

◄ NOBBY STILES: FORD CORSAIR

Born in Collyhurst, Manchester, in 1942, midfield dynamo Norbert 'Nobby' Stiles enjoyed 14 glorious years at Old Trafford between 1957 and 1971. He won League Championship winners' medals in 1965 and 1967, and a World Cup winners' medal in 1966, followed by a European Cup winners' medal in 1968. Stiles, an avid fan of United since a schoolboy, made his first-team debut in October 1960 against Bolton Wanderers. The local lad established himself as a regular, making 31 appearances during his first season.

His tackling was fierce and he was known for his aggressive style on the pitch which made him a midfield fixture for Busby's United and Alf Ramsey's England.

He joined Preston in 1973 as Bobby Charlton's assistant, after two years at Middlesbrough. He managed Preston and West Bromwich Albion, but made a bigger mark with the United youth set-up where his spell between 1989 and 1993 coincided with the emergence of Beckham, Butt, Giggs, Scholes and the Nevilles.

as a central defender who was cool-headed under pressure, and helped the club win the 1965 and 1967 First Division Football League championships as well as the 1968 European Cup. (Sadler scored in the Semi-Final against Real Madrid to help United to the Wembley showcase.)

Sadler left United in 1973 after playing 272 league games to join Preston North End. He later became manager of a Manchester building society branch before joining former team-mate Bobby Charlton in Old Trafford corporate hospitality. As well as commenting on United in the media, he is currently secretary of the Manchester United Former Players' Association.

▲ DAVID HERD: VOLVO P1800

Born in Moss Side in 1934, David Herd was the son of a former Manchester City player. He started footballing life as an amateur alongside his dad at Stockport County age 15, moving to Arsenal in 1954 where he registered an impressive 99 goals in 166 matches. After seeing him finish second to Jimmy Greaves in the First Division scoring table in 1961, Matt Busby paid £40,000 for his services and he formed a very effective spearhead with Denis Law. His standout season was 1965-66, when he hit the net 32 times.

Herd, who uniquely scored on his United debuts in the FA Cup, League Cup and all three European competitions, struggled with injury after breaking a leg in 1966, and left for Stoke weeks after the European Cup Final. Though he missed the Final itself, Herd was awarded a winners' medal for his part in United's memorable campaign.

A subsequent management career took in Waterford and Lincoln City, but Herd will best be remembered for a haul of 145 goals in 265 appearances in a red shirt – a strike rate of better than one in two that stacks up against any United great, past or present.

► DAVID SADLER: ROVER P6

Utility player David Sadler (born in Kent in 1946) started his professional career with Manchester United in 1963, having signed from non-league Maidstone (where, coincidentally, current Red Chris Smalling started his career) on his 17th birthday. He played in almost all outfield roles during his 11 seasons at Old Trafford, excelling

GEORGE BEST: MINI, E-TYPE JAGUAR, ROLLS-ROYCE, LOTUS EUROPA

George Best was as promiscuous with his cars as he was with his girlfriends, flitting between iconic Sixties Mini Cooper (left), Jaguar (above, with Swedish girlfriend Siv Hederby), Rolls-Royce (top right) and Lotus (right). The Mini Cooper was a particular favourite: he retained it until his death in 2005 and it was among the exhibits in a commemorative 2008 exhibition in Ballymena, County Antrim, alongside caps he won for Northern Ireland and the Benfica top he wore after swapping shirts when United won the European Cup in 1968.

▶ THE STRIKING VIKING

George Best and Eva Haraldsted, perched on the boot of his striking Lotus Europa, on the occasion of their 'engagement' in October 1969. The Danish girl had caught Best's eye on a pre-season tour in Copenhagen and the press had jumped on the bandwagon, dubbing Eva the 'Striking Viking'. They arranged for her to come to England where she promptly announced their engagement, but Best broke it off soon after and made history as being the last person in England to be sued for breach of promise to marry.

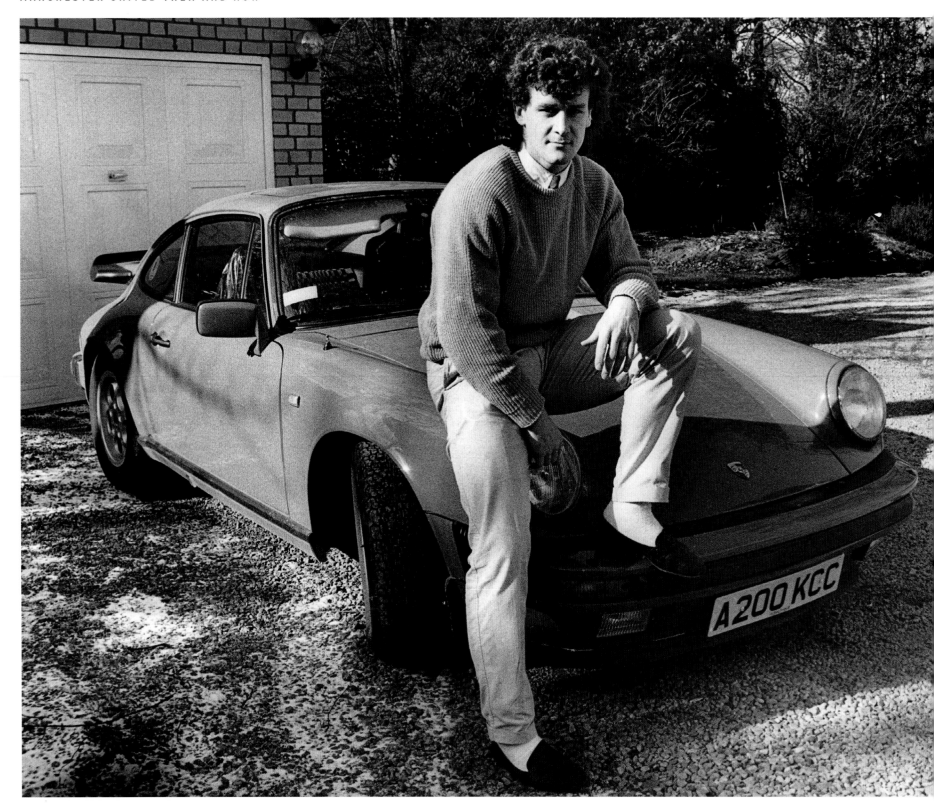

◄ MARK HUGHES'S PORSCHE

Young, free and single, 22-year-old Leslie Mark Hughes poses with his Porsche 911 sports car outside his bachelor residence in Bowden, near Altrincham, in February 1986.

Hughes (born 1963) signed as a professional with United in November 1980 and made his League Cup debut exactly three years later. Manager Ron Atkinson sold him to Barcelona in 1986, but he didn't settle in Spain and was loaned to Bayern Munich. Alex Ferguson re-signed him for £1.8 million (then a club record) in 1988 and he was voted PFA Player of the Year in 1989 and 1991 – the first player to win it twice. Hughes went on to win his second FA Cup, the European Cup Winners' Cup against former team Barcelona and the League Cup. His strike partnership with Eric Cantona helped United to their first league title for 26 years but the arrival of Andy Cole in 1995 marked the end of 15 years at United and he left for Chelsea for £1.5 million. In 1998 he moved to Southampton and managed to collect 14 yellow cards in his first season, a Premiership record. Following further spells at Everton and then Blackburn Rovers he finally hung up his playing boots in 2002 at age 39. Hughes has enjoyed managerial success with Wales, Blackburn Rovers, Manchester City and Fulham.

► RIO'S ASTON MARTIN

Rio Ferdinand's Aston Martin Vanquish S, registration 100 RF, typifies the status symbol cars of the modern footballer. He used the plate on an Aston Martin DB-7 when joining United from Leeds for a record UK fee (for a defender) of £30 million in 2002. Wayne Rooney also had a Vanquish, but sold it for £150,000 complete with personalised plate WAZ 8 in 2008.

▼ ROONEY'S BENTLEY

With United receiving sponsorship from Audi, it's not surprising that Wayne Rooney's 2011 car of choice was an Audi RS6 in United red. One of United's most flamboyant car drivers has been Portuguese winger Luis Nani who owns a Lamborghini Gallardo, one of a limited edition of 250 in the world. Wayne Rooney has had an impressive fleet of cars over the years which have included a BMW X5, Mercedes CLK, Cadillac Escalade and a Chrysler 300C. Ryan Giggs, former goalkeeper Edwin van der Sar and Rooney all have been Bentley Continental owners. In 2008 Wayne narrowly escaped collecting a parking ticket for his Bentley when he went shopping in Manchester with wife Coleen. At an estimated weekly salary of £140,000 plus bonuses he wouldn't have needed time to pay.

▼ RONALDO'S VERY USED FERRARI

In 2009 United's Portuguese superstar winger Cristiano Ronaldo escaped unhurt after crashing his Ferrari sports car in a tunnel near Manchester airport on the way to training. The car was badly damaged but 23-year-old Ronaldo was not injured. United goalkeeper Edwin van der Sar was travelling behind Ronaldo at the wheel of his Bentley, the pair travelling from homes in Cheshire to United's Carrington training complex. Ronaldo replaced his Ferrari with a slightly more conservative Audi R8 from United's official suppliers, its price tag a 'modest' £70,000.

TRAINING REGIMES

◄ TRAINING AT BLACKPOOL

Taking the squad to soak up the sea air at Blackpool before important matches was a regular practice in the Fifties, though this 1957 photograph suggests a local youngster has decided to try his luck with a few squat jumps behind Bobby Charlton and Wilf McGuinness. The squad would often go on to stay at the 400-room Norbreck Hydro (inset) on the Blackpool seafront, a favoured venue when United visited the resort. Built as a private country house, it was purchased around the end of the 19th century by businessman J.H. Shorrocks who expanded the building in several phases, adding a ballroom, swimming pool and solarium. It is now the Norbreck Castle Hotel.

◄ ANY OLD KIT

Sir Matt with his senior players, Bobby Charlton, Denis Law, George Best, Brian Kidd, Pat Crerand and David Sadler pose outside the Cliff training ground with Busby in January 1971. The motley selection of training kit on show reflects the fact that training was far from the regimented, closely monitored process it has become in the current century. The only common factor appears to be Adidas footwear. The photo call was no doubt arranged to show support for their old manager just days after he had resumed control on 29 December 1970. While Matt Busby was relatively hands-on in training his players, he also had coaches and trainers who worked with him. These included the long-serving Jimmy Murphy, ex-goalkeeper Jack Crompton and, latterly, former Busby Babe Wilf McGuinness. One of Sandy Busby's complaints about the BBC drama *United*, which portrayed the events around the Munich disaster, was that it portrayed his father as someone who never put on a tracksuit and spent time coaching the players.

TODAY

Manchester United's training regime in 2011 may appear informal, with Sir Alex Ferguson happy to clown for the cameras with star striker Wayne Rooney before their Champions League Semi-Final against Schalke. But the methods used are cutting-edge.

Manager Ferguson has often credited his former assistant, Portuguese coach Carlos Queiroz, who enjoyed two stints with United between 2002-03 and 2004-08, with introducing advanced training methods at United. This includes computerised analysis of opponents, via a 'ProZone' system, which allows training to be set up to simulate match conditions more closely.

In the 2009-10 season United became the first Premier League club to adopt the GPS (Global Positioning System) tracking device. Worn inside training vests alongside a heart-rate monitor, the device shows how far and how fast players have run. Players can go into the sports science department after training and find out their data straightaway.

THE CLIFF TRAINING GROUND

EX-RUGBY LEAGUE

The Cliff is Carrington's much smaller, but much older antecedent and was the place where future United legends from Duncan Edwards and Bobby Charlton to Ryan Giggs, Gary Neville, Paul Scholes and David Beckham first honed their skills.

It was originally home to Rugby League outfit Broughton Rangers before United, buoyed by new owner and benefactor James Gibson, arrived at the facilities in 1938, with Broughton moving on to the nearby Belle Vue greyhound racetrack. The facilities were initially used as a home for the club's newly formed youth development team, the Manchester United Junior Athletic Club.

It took two decades for United's first team to begin training full-time at the Cliff but soon after they arrived the club bought the lease of the land and quickly began constructing a then state-of-the-art training complex.

Old versions of the Cliff are the backdrop to some of the images in the book including photos of Matt Busby (on page 48) where the old grandstand can be seen behind, or more obviously on page 106.

▶ WEIGHT TRAINING

Weight training and stomach crunches were the order of the day at the Cliff before the advent of fitness coaches, nutritionists and powered treadmills.

▼ TOO SMALL, TOO PUBLIC

As the new millennium approached, it became apparent that the Cliff's amenities were not quite up to standard. With that in mind, Sir Alex Ferguson advocated a move away to a new, purpose-built complex nearby. It would become United's Trafford Training Centre at Carrington.

Ferguson was concerned at the openness of the Cliff's ground where fans and opposition informants alike could watch United train. A fair point, perhaps, but fans would forever mourn a lost golden era where they could rub shoulders with their heroes.

With the first team gone, many assumed that the Cliff would go the way of football stadia when its club vacates – fall into disrepair or become a block of flats. Fittingly, however, the Cliff returned to its roots and is now home to the youngest of United's hopefuls, as well as being the hub of the club's community schemes.

THE CLIFF TRAINING GROUND

BACK FROM THE BEACH IN JULY

United players, including Paddy Crerand and Alex Stepney (on the left with George Best partially visible behind them), and Bobby Charlton and Tony Dunne (together on right), gather at the Cliff at the start of the season, July 1972. A footballer's average summer break from the game then was longer than their present-day counterparts, with revenue-earning pre-season tours not yet on the agenda. Coach Malcolm Musgrove talks to the players while Manager Frank O'Farrell (on left, back to camera) waits to speak. O'Farrell had come to Old Trafford after guiding Leicester City to promotion, but would only preside over two pre-season meetings, giving way to Tommy Docherty in December 1972. One of his problems was dealing with George Best, who had a special relationship with Matt Busby and would prove ungovernable by any successor. O'Farrell's way of dealing with the superstars he inherited was to make them schedule appointments to see him. This impersonal approach was a deliberate contrast to Wilf McGuinness, the former coach who inherited the manager's job from Busby and had been unable to establish any distance or authority.

▲ 2003

National coach Sven-Goran Eriksson addresses the England squad at the Cliff in November 2003. With Wembley in the process of being remodelled, the friendly international with Denmark was staged at Old Trafford, hence the use of United's old training ground. Note the adverts installed to take advantage of TV coverage of training sessions.

◄ TODAY

One of the organisations that uses the Cliff today is Kickz, a Football Foundation project launched in 2006 that aims to use the appeal of professional football clubs to create safer, stronger and more respectful communities by developing young people's potential. Each Premier League club runs Kickz in partnership with the local police, aiming to engage disadvantaged young people from the local area and encourage them to move on to volunteer and take qualifications.

CARRINGTON

◄ CARRINGTON MOSS

Carrington Moss, as its name suggests, is a peat bog close to the River Mersey some 10 miles south-west of Manchester. The city has long used it as a dumping ground for waste and, during World War II it was used as a 'Starfish' site, an area used to simulate the streets of Manchester as a decoy for enemy bombers. In the immediate postwar period its role was reversed and the picture from Manchester City Council Local Image Collection, taken in August 1946, shows it being used as an army ammunition dump.

TRAFFORD TRAINING CENTRE

Though known to many – United fans or otherwise – as simply Carrington, the Trafford Training Centre is the Reds' all-purpose state-of-the-art training facility. It was originally viewed as a new complex for a new millennium. United arriving as European champions, though the main building wasn't officially opened until the summer of 2000.

Whereas their old training home, the Cliff, was renowned for its openness and revered by fans that occasionally got to witness their team train and

regularly catch glimpses of their idols, Carrington is the complete opposite. Known to some as 'fortress Carrington', it is intensely private (unless a press call has been arranged, as above) and shrouded by a cloak of trees and tall wire fences, such is the media intrusion and high stakes surrounding the modern game.

Inside the site, which covers more than 100 acres, are a myriad of amenities to enable United sides to gun for trophies on a regular basis. Among the facilities are swimming pools, saunas, gyms, a TV studio for MUTV and no fewer than 14 training pitches. With a workforce of more than 200, including everyone from physiotherapists, sports scientists, and dieticians to chefs, Carrington really is a world of its own – it even boasts its own sewage system! So it is perhaps fitting that the complex was originally the idea of United's most successful manager, Sir Alex Ferguson.

In May 2011, an £11.5 million extension was approved, including a two-storey extension to the main building, a new two-storey building for staff and visitors, two enclosed training pitches and an additional building for spectators. There will also be a new security lodge, and an extended car park with two entrances and exits – one exclusively for the players.

▲ GPS TRACKER

Park Ji-Sung wearing the GPS training vest that provides important data to the United sports science department. The South Korean international was training on 3 May 2011 ahead of the Champions League second leg against Schalke at Old Trafford. Park ultimately didn't start the game and was rested by Sir Alex Ferguson for what he considered a more important game, the Sunday home fixture against Chelsea. The subsequent victory over Chelsea all but handed United the 2010-11 title.

FA CUP 1963

FA CUP 1963

United's post-Munich rebuilding process would last a decade, and would be the ultimate tribute to those lost in the crash. The new team would be built around three future United legends – George Best, Denis Law and Bobby Charlton. Charlton had made his debut for United in 1954, and survived the Munich disaster with only minor injuries.

The nucleus of this side – minus Best, who was yet to make his first-team debut – captured their first silverware in the form of the FA Cup in 1963, a 3-1 victory over Leicester City that gave them their second win in Busby's managerial reign (the first was 15 years earlier in 1948). The Duke of Edinburgh, who was introduced to the teams before the game (above), had also presented the cup on United's last visit to Wembley in 1958 when they lost to Bolton.

United's league campaign had been poor (they'd finished 19th), and Leicester had done the double over them. Indeed the midlanders had been tipped to do the league and cup double under another respected Scots manager, Matt Gillies, before falling away. The Final took place on 25 May, three weeks later than scheduled, reflecting the fact that the season had been disrupted by a particularly severe winter, also known as the 'Big Freeze'.

While United's keeper Dave Gaskell started nervily, making three fumbles in the first quarter of an hour, it was the usually reliable Leicester goalkeeper, Gordon Banks – who'd received his first England cap weeks before – who was culpable in all three goals; a throw-out was intercepted by Pat Crerand for Law to open the scoring, he parried a Charlton shot at David Herd's feet, then finally dropped the ball for Herd to seal victory with the third United goal. Leicester's Keyworth headed a consolation that had reduced the arrears to 3-1, but on the day United were never seriously threatened.

Having won the toss of a coin, United wore their traditional red. Leicester played in white as their usual combination of blue shirts and white shorts would have been indistinguishable from the opposition on black and white television. Attendance at the Empire Stadium, as it was then known, was 99,604.

The FA Cup travelled back to Manchester by train via St. Pancras Station (pictured below in the hands of skipper Noel Cantwell). It was the first major silverware for six years for Matt Busby but would not be his last. Cantwell was hoisted onto team-mates Albert Quixall and Pat Crerand's shoulders after the presentation, but the pair were told to put him down as, in those days, the national anthem was played at this point (see above); it was switched in future years to precede the kick-off.

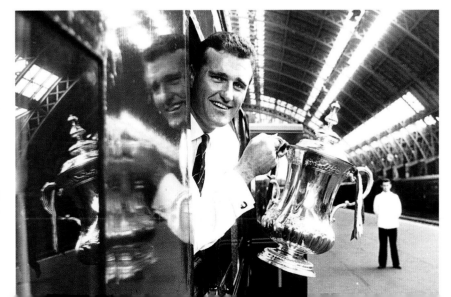

EUROPEAN CUP 1968

STORY OF 1968

The European Cup remained Matt Busby's ultimate goal – but following the decimation of the first team squad at Munich, it would take until 1965-66 for United to qualify again. (These were the days when only the champions were allowed to participate under the one-club-per-country rule.)

As in 1958, United got to the Semi-Final but could only muster a lone Stiles strike as they went out at the hands of Partizan Belgrade. Their next attempt to claim Europe's top club prize would be successful, however, beating Hibernian Malta, Sarajevo and Gornik Zabrze en route to a Semi-Final showdown with Real Madrid.

A slender 1-0 lead was established at Old Trafford before United battled out a 3-3 draw in the Bernabéu to earn themselves a place in the Final. Their opponents at Wembley were Portuguese champions Benfica, whom United had humbled in the Quarter-Final two years earlier, George Best outshining European Footballer of the Year Eusébio.

This time the star was unlikely: John Aston, who repeatedly passed Benfica's Adolfo on the left wing to spray crosses to the strikers. Bobby Charlton – apart from Foulkes, the only Munich survivor on the pitch – opened the scoring in the second half before Jaime Graca equalised. Extra time saw goals from George Best, teenage birthday boy Brian Kidd (a replacement for the injured Denis Law) and a second for Charlton bring the trophy to England for the first time.

Just over a decade on from Munich, Matt Busby had honoured the memories of those who perished and conquered Europe for the first time. The decade had seen the making of not only a football club but a sporting legend.

▶ KIDD COMES OF AGE

Playing in the showcase Final was a dream come true for 19-year-old Brian Kidd, a United supporter who had signed schoolboy forms five years earlier. Good form in United's reserves saw Matt Busby grant him a debut at the start of the 1967-68 season in the Charity Shield as substitute for the injured David Herd. From then on, Kidd's form kept him in the side for all but four matches. As he scored the third of United's four goals, fans sung the Beatles classic 'Hello, Goodbye' with the chorus modified to 'Eusébio, and I say Kiddo'. That European Cup medal was to be his only honour at United, however, and he moved to Arsenal for £110,000 after the Reds' relegation to the Second Division in 1974.

▶ INSPIRATION FROM THE BOSS

Manager Matt Busby delivers words of inspiration at the end of normal time as United, pegged back by a late equaliser, redouble their efforts to secure their first European Cup. In those days there was only one substitute per side, in United's case unused goalkeeper Jimmy Rimmer (who would win the European Cup with Aston Villa in 1982). Coach Wilf McGuinness was also inspirational. 'Look, they've gone, they're knackered,' he said to all who would listen, telling Nobby Stiles, who had run endlessly in his effort to contain Eusébio: 'Come on, Nob, another half an hour and you're home.' Stiles and Bobby Charlton had both won after extra time in England's 1966 World Cup win.

▶ THE ULTIMATE ACHIEVEMENT

Bobby Charlton and Matt Busby share in the celebrations, having suffered the agony of Munich 10 years earlier. Centre-half Bill Foulkes was the other survivor of the crash to play a part on the pitch that May 1968 day. Looking back on that day, Sir Bobby told the *Independent*'s James Lawton, 'This was unquestionably the pinnacle of Busby's football life. For days he had been reminded of the meaning of the game, the legacy of Munich and how his boys had died in pursuit of this trophy. So many people believed that this night was for him and about him and it was natural, I suppose, that everyone wanted to touch him at the end of the game. Even though I was so tired, when I got to him I started dragging people off him. I said, "Give him some room".'

ALBERT SQUARE 1968

OUTDOING THE NEIGHBOURS

United's open-top bus is escorted into crowded Albert Square by mounted police as thousands turn out to mark their historic European Cup victory. Neighbours Manchester City had just won the league title for the second time, but failed to inspire such scenes of public rejoicing. (United finished second, just two points – a win in those days – behind.) Not all the United heroes were able to take a well-deserved bow. Bobby Charlton and Nobby Stiles, for instance, had to report for England duty and missed the homecoming.

TODAY

Albert Square was modernised in 1987. The road through its eastern side, past Manchester Town Hall, was pedestrianised and trees were planted. Consequently, the route taken by the open-top bus in 1968 is no longer available as traffic runs through the opposite side of the square. Almost one million fans took to the streets of Manchester when United paraded through the city following the club's outstanding treble success of 1999 – the Premiership, the FA Cup and the Champions League (European Cup). The red side of the City of Manchester turned out in force to witness a scene they had been denied for a decade. United were the only English side to have won the European Cup at this time, and followed Glasgow Celtic as winners.

It would be 31 years before they claimed their second European Cup, a third victory coming in the all-English Champions League Final of 2008. But plans to repeat the parade following the win over Chelsea in Moscow were scuppered, after recent city-centre violence involving Rangers fans following their UEFA Cup Final defeat against Zenit St Petersburg at Eastlands.

In 2011, Manchester came to a standstill twice in seven days, the authorities granting City and United permission for open-top bus parades to mark their respective FA Cup and Premier League title triumphs.

WARWICK ROAD ON MATCH DAY

GETTING A GOOD PLACE ON THE TERRACES

Fans walk down Warwick Road to Old Trafford on match day. The relatively formal dress of jackets, the near-total dominance of the male sex and the lack of club colours worn differentiates these spectators in 1960 from today's matchgoers. The roadside landscape has changed significantly too, Old Trafford barely peeking over the cafeteria in the centre of the shot. Before the advent of all-seater stadia it was important to get to the ground early and get a good position on the terraces, or a good seat in the stand, hence the several figures running towards the ground.

TODAY

It was fitting that Sir Matt Busby was alive to witness Warwick Road North named in his honour in 1993. Though United's first great manager died less than a year later, the road that runs along Old Trafford's world-famous façade now pays tribute to the man that brought United's first European Cup to the stadium. This contemporary shot shows a casually dressed and more cosmopolitan crowd, with the East Stand towering over them as they approach the much-vaunted 'Theatre of Dreams'. With the vast majority of seats occupied by season ticket holders, and all seats allocated, there is no rush to get a good position. The few-thousand match tickets that are available to home fans begin to be sold approximately six weeks before the game. With demand outstripping supply – for home and away fans – the extra tickets are offered to supporters' club members on a lottery basis, resulting in many disappointed fans. For them, the move to develop the South Stand cannot come quick enough.

RED DEVILS SHOP

SOUVENIRS APLENTY

This view of the Red Devils shop shows that photographs and badges were the greatest money-spinners in the era between the rattle and rosette and the replica shirt. It's likely that United's current online operation turns over more money in a few days than this shop took in a year, but the dedication of the staff shines through in the photo on the right. The Red Devils shop was initially owned by the Busby family and was situated in a small hut near to the railway line that runs alongside the ground, but the club soon recognised the revenue potential from merchandising and relocated the facility to somewhere more suitable. Posters of Bobby Charlton and George Best adorn the windows (left), while the proximity of car parking to the stadium is a sign of considerably less congested and traffic-managed times.

TODAY: MUFC MEGASTORE

Situated in Old Trafford's East Stand and opened in 2000, Manchester United's retail store (below right) is not too far from the old Red Devils shop. The 17,000 square-feet Megastore ties in with the operation of stadium tours and the Manchester United museum and is a seven-day-a-week tourist attraction and money-spinner. As football merchandising has evolved, the range of gifts and turnover has increased exponentially. United boasts the store has more than 800 types of gifts on the shelves from shirts through mousemats to slippers, and millions pass through its mammoth 39 checkouts every year.

With many millions of fans scattered across the globe, it's no surprise to see Manchester United merchandise almost everywhere you look. Hats, scarves and the famous red shirts are just three items in a lucrative worldwide industry that helped the club make more than £280 million in revenue during the 2009-10 season.

Such is the global pulling power of Premier League football clubs that many teams now undertake pre-season tours in different parts of the world not only to broaden their fanbase but also to strengthen their merchandising arm. Manchester United is no exception and has participated in visits to the United States, Asia and Africa.

The gravy train shows no sign of stopping; commercial activities accounted for nearly a third of United's total revenue. Nike's best-selling football shirt has sold an average of 1.5 million units worldwide every season since 2005 and the club sits just behind Spanish duo Barcelona and serial leaders Real Madrid in Deloitte's annual football rich list for the 2009-10 season.

OLD TRAFFORD STADIUM:
1930-1949

AERIAL VIEW 1930

As the club's financial foundations strengthened during the Twenties, the directors found themselves in the position to buy the Old Trafford freehold from Manchester Breweries in March 1927 for the sum of £21,350 (that included unpaid rent). Having been freed from the £1,300 annual rent and rates payments, United were now able to reap the benefits of any improvements to the stadium in full. The death of John Davies the same year, however – coupled with the Great Depression at the end of the decade – saw supporters questioning why the club was constructing a new road alongside the Popular Side of the ground rather than investing in the team.

This was an especially relevant point for them to raise in view of the fact that United made the worst ever start to a top-flight campaign in August 1930 when they failed to earn a single point from their first 12 league games before the season ended with relegation to the Second Division.

While John Davies' decision to develop Old Trafford amid the industrial zone alongside the Ship Canal and docks seemed like a good idea at the time, the advent of World War II meant that the stadium was hemmed in by German bombing targets. Inevitably, some of these incendiaries missed their intended targets and landed on Old Trafford causing massive devastation to the Main Stand. Football had continued to be played during the first years of the hostilities with league and cup competitions set up as a means to keep the civilian population in good spirits but this came to an end at Old Trafford in March 1941 and it would take many years for the club to rebuild the stadium.

1948: NO SOUTH STAND

The financial strain of the war years meant that United had to wait for government compensation to return Old Trafford to anywhere near its former glory. Grants were allocated in August 1945 to clear the ground and November 1946 to demolish what was left of the Main Stand, but it wasn't until March 1948 that funds were made available and required permits agreed to begin the reconstruction of the stand and terraces. This refurbishment was quickly carried out and league football returned to Old Trafford with the visit of Bolton Wanderers in August 1949 (right and below).

1949: GIBSON'S AMBITION REALISED

United's benefactor, James W. Gibson, who had amassed a vast personal fortune through the manufacture of army uniforms during World War I, was responsible for pushing forward the rebuilding agenda. He was instrumental in persuading the Government into agreeing financial support for the 10 clubs whose stadiums were in need of rebuilding work because of bomb damage. Gibson's memory is commemorated on plaques in the players' tunnel and above the railway bridge in Sir Matt Busby Way. He died of a heart attack in 1951 and his widow, Lillian, remained the largest shareholder until her own death in 1971. Thankfully he lived long enough to see the return to Old Trafford for the start of the 1949-50 season.

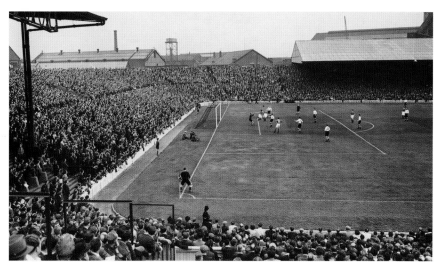

OLD TRAFFORD STADIUM: DAWN OF THE SIXTIES

◄ TURNSTILES IN 1960

With memories of World War II damage confined to the history books as the club once again enjoyed unhindered use of Old Trafford from 1954 onwards, the development of Old Trafford continued apace throughout the Fifties with the board, in September 1957, announcing their intention to increase capacity to a massive 100,000 and extend the cover on the Popular Side. The tragedy the following February changed these plans somewhat, although an increase in the number of fans – especially youngsters – following the Munich disaster led to extra turnstiles being installed in the Stretford End. The directors embraced new technology in their quest to redevelop Old Trafford as the best stadium in the country. Southampton had been the first club to install permanent floodlights at their ground in 1950 but the Football League initially refused to sanction their use. They eventually relented, with the first floodlit league match taking place at Fratton Park in February 1956 between Portsmouth and Newcastle. United were quick to take up the same option. Floodlights were soon installed in all four corners of the ground and, first used for the visit of Bolton Wanderers in March 1957, have seen regular use thereby allowing the club to stage evening games.

► NOBBY AND THE SCOREBOARD END

Nobby Stiles poses in front of the Scoreboard End as it looked in 1960. While it would cost three shillings and sixpence (17.5p) for covered standing, in 1960 you could watch from the uncovered lower standing for two shillings and sixpence (12.5p). Programmes cost fourpence (2p) increasing in 1962 to sixpence (2.5p). Season tickets could be had for the price of £7 or £8 and 10 shillings (£8.50p). The Sixties was the decade when professional footballers began to enjoy increased wages. The Professional Footballers' Association played a pivotal role in the abolition of the £20 minimum wage in 1961 and many clubs were faced with financial difficulties in raising the funds necessary to develop their grounds. United were no exception and – with falling attendances – launched the Manchester United Development Association the same year. This group contributed towards the cost of installing further seating in the Stretford End which had been covered in 1959. Other modifications to the ground included repairing the Paddock the following year, as well as refurbishing the roof of the United Road (North Stand) section in 1961.

► TODAY

The last time you could pay just £1 to stand and watch United was the 1978-79 campaign. Season tickets first topped the £100 mark in 1986-87, rising to £320 in 1994-95 and up to £456 in 2000-01. In 2010-11 a season ticket in The East Stand varied between £513 for East Stand Lower to £684 for East Stand Upper.

OLD TRAFFORD STADIUM REBUILDING

GEARING UP FOR THE CUP

Old Trafford has been the subject of a continuous rebuilding process over the years, and never more so than in the Sixties. The team Busby built was so attractive that larger crowds were attracted as the decade progressed, encouraging the club to increase its capacity to meet demand. United chiefs spent nearly half a million pounds on preparing Old Trafford as a World Cup venue in 1966, of which the

pictured works were early evidence. Old Trafford hosted Group Three in partnership with Everton's Goodison Park. The national teams of Portugal, Hungary and Bulgaria all graced the pitch, though the fourth, Brazil, played all their games in Liverpool. Goodison also hosted a Quarter- and Semi-Final.

A CHANGE OF SCALE

Formerly known as the Scoreboard End, the East Stand was redeveloped in time for the new millennium and houses the away fans as well as catering for disabled supporters. The structure can hold approximately 12,000 people. The first capacity audience in the East Stand saw David Beckham score the only goal of the Premier League match against Middlesbrough in January 2000.

When Old Trafford was divided into alphabetical sections, the East Stand – where a particularly vocal congregation earned themselves a reputation with their chants and songs – was allocated the letter K and is therefore also known as the

K Stand. This building boasts a tinted glass façade and also houses the club's administrative offices as well as the production hub of the official website and magazine. The exterior of the stand is often used for screening adverts and images but has also been the backdrop against which the 50th anniversary memorials of Munich took place. At the final home match of the 2011 season, United were able to display one important number in the glass front of the East Stand before receiving the Barclays Premiership trophy. The number was 19. They were now ahead of rivals Liverpool who had won 18 league titles.

OLD TRAFFORD STADIUM: FIRST OF THE CANTILEVERS

◄ 1966 AND ALL THAT

FIFA had awarded the 1966 World Cup to England in August 1960, with the victors fending off challenges from West Germany and Spain. By 1963, the FA had decided on their chosen venues for the tournament with Old Trafford being selected to share Group Three matches with Goodison Park and United embarked on an ambitious three-year reconstruction of the ground aided by a £40,000 grant.

Other modifications to bring Old Trafford up to scratch for the World Cup included rebuilding the corner paddocks while in the Main Stand, facilities – including camera platforms, phone lines and interview rooms – for up to 400 journalists were included when planning the remodelling of the stadium.

This aerial photo is from 22 May 1966. Two days later, an auspicious event happened in the history of United – Eric Cantona was born.

► UNDER CONSTRUCTION IN 1965

From left to right, Denis Law, Pat Dunne, Paddy Crerand, George Best and Tony Dunne in training at Old Trafford, 1965. Construction of the cantilever stand to replace the old United Road Stand – now the North Stand – began in the 1964 close season. The design of the new stand (by Mather and Nutter, now called Atherden Fuller) negated the need for pillars thereby giving fans an unobstructed view of the pitch. Completed at a cost of £350,000, the stand catered for 20,000 spectators and was organised so that those who preferred standing were nearer the pitch while those who chose to be seated were higher up. The stand also boasted the first private boxes at any British football ground, an idea that Matt Busby had first seen in the United States.

► THE SCOREBOARD END GETS A ROOF

Sammy McIlroy shoots, watched by Brian Kidd (left) and Alan Gowling (right) as United lose to Wolves in January 1972. George Best had been banned by manager Frank O'Farrell that week for skipping training and had been seen out with Miss Great Britain, Carolyn Moore.

In those days the Scoreboard End had a low picket fence behind the goal painted in red and white sections and was still the place where the away fans were located. Most significant, though, is the construction of the cantilever stand behind the playing action. This stand would rise higher than the old terracing, replace the scoreboard and would last until the development of the East Stand in the 21st century.

OLD TRAFFORD STADIUM:
THE TUNNEL

OLD TRAFFORD STADIUM: THE TUNNEL

Many famous players have led United teams out over the decades – none more so than lifelong servant Bobby Charlton (left) – and the majority emerged into the Old Trafford arena from the original players' tunnel. Situated in the middle of the Main South Stand, all the greats of English football in the Fifties and Sixties walked out here. The tunnel was deemed surplus to requirements as Old Trafford changed in the Nineties but still remains as the only surviving part of the original stadium designed by the esteemed Archibald Leitch a century ago. As part of the ground centenary celebrations in March 2010, a time capsule was buried at the entrance to the original tunnel. Fans who had been lucky enough to get tickets for the visit of Fulham were treated to a replica of the first ever Old Trafford match programme while the club had traced relatives of all those involved in that match with Liverpool in February 1910 and invited them to the ceremony. Unfortunately, they were unable to locate relatives of Billy Meredith, Dick Duckworth and Ernest Mangnall.

There was a warm Old Trafford welcome for a returning son in 1972 after Nobby Stiles (above) had been sold to Middlesbrough. United were drawn against Boro in the 1972 FA Cup and the banners were hung out to celebrate Stiles' first playing return. Nobby went on to join Charlton at Preston North End in the mid-Seventies and, after management spells with Preston and West Brom, returned to Old Trafford in 1989. Many products of his all-conquering youth team made a vital contribution to the club's quest for success under Alex Ferguson.

▼ TODAY

A noticeable change to the layout occurred in the mid-Nineties when the players' tunnel was relocated as a result of modernisation works carried out to the dressing rooms. The new entrance now emerges from the south-west corner of the ground and the players walk out onto the pitch protected by a concertina tunnel.

OLD TRAFFORD STADIUM:
FENCING THE STRETFORD END

END OF AN ERA

It was the end of an era in more ways than one. While the 1973-74 season will always be remembered as the last time that Manchester United were relegated from the top flight, it was also notorious for other unwanted reasons. In a worrying trend that seemed to be magnifying, fans had started to invade the pitch. It had happened at a friendly at home to Glasgow Rangers in March 1974 – where 77 fans were arrested – and occurred again in the final home game of the league campaign the following month...the Manchester derby (above).

As it turned out, former Old Trafford favourite Denis Law scored the only goal of the game for the visitors but results elsewhere had already confirmed United's relegation to the Second Division for the first time since before World War II. Club officials pleaded with the perpetrators to return to the stands so that the match could be finished but to no avail and referee David Smith had no option other than to abandon the fixture with four minutes still to play.

The biggest failing of the campaign from United's point of view was a lack of goals scored. The team failed to score in 20 of their 42 league matches and Sammy McIlroy finished the season as the club's top scorer with a paltry six goals.

▲ THE FENCES GO UP

The FA were alarmed by the events at Old Trafford and accepted the club's decision to install nine-foot fences in an attempt to prevent any repeat performance. Football violence involving home and away fans had become a fact of life in English football and fences went up around the major football grounds in the top tier.

United kicked off the 1974-75 campaign with the Stetford End incarcerated. The photo (above) shows the first home match in August 1974 against Millwall. Their sojourn in the Second Division lasted just one season, however, as United – helped by double-figure scoring tallies from Lou Macari, Gerry Daly and the newly signed Stuart Pearson – powered to the championship crown, losing just seven games during the process.

▶ TODAY

The disaster at Hillsborough in April 1989 prompted Lord Justice Taylor to recommend the removal of the fences that had become a necessary part of the game for half a generation and the conversion of Premiership stadia to all-seater. While hooliganism has not been completely eradicated from football, it is often confined to high-profile European games where the troublemakers are not known to police and any trouble occurs outside of the stadium. The average football fan of the 21st century is also older than they were in the Seventies and at United the proportion of casual fans has diminished considerably. The Stretford End is free of the fences that once closed it in.

OLD TRAFFORD STADIUM: POST HILLSBOROUGH

◄ STRETFORD END BECOMES ALL-SEATER

The repercussions that followed the Hillsborough disaster in April 1989 – where 96 Liverpool fans lost their lives during an FA Cup Semi-Final against Nottingham Forest – and the ensuing report into ground safety in the wake of the tragedy were felt at football clubs all around the country. The Taylor Report recommended that all stadia for clubs in the top two tiers of English football should become all-seater by the 1994-95 season and this had an inevitable impact on Old Trafford. The Stretford End housed the main standing area of the ground but was demolished during the summer of 1992 (left) to make way for a £10 million cantilevered stand that was officially renamed the West Stand.

► MAKE WAY FOR THE NEW NORTH STAND

By the mid-Nineties, the club had come to the conclusion that the stadium did not have a big enough capacity to accommodate all the fans who wanted to watch their team in action. United, therefore, announced the construction of a new North Stand in 1995. It was to be a three-tiered cantilever stand that could house more than 25,000 spectators in comfort and was built at a cost of £28 million (almost a third of which was spent on purchasing the additional land necessary to build the behemoth). The new North Stand also included executive suites and boxes as well as going on to house the club's impressive museum.

► THE ALMOST FINISHED NORTH STAND

The North Stand would boast the biggest cantilever roof in Europe and incorporated new floodlights along the roof. Many clubs – including United and Liverpool – dismantled their traditional floodlights in the early Nineties and replaced them with less obtrusive counterparts. This was facilitated by the fact that there were no longer any open terraces or low stands that did not allow the necessary lighting to be sited at the optimum height above the pitch. By the time Old Trafford came to staging its second major international tournament (Euro 96) it boasted a capacity of 55,000.

INTO THE 21ST CENTURY

▲ PASSING THE 76,000 MARK

The final years of the 20th century and the first decade of the new millennium saw yet more redevelopment of Old Trafford with a second tier being added to the East Stand. It increased the ground's capacity to approximately 61,000 when it was opened in January 2000, a figure that was pushed nearer the 70,000 mark when a second tier was added to the West Stand. That was built for the 2000-01 season and brought the ground's total seating to just over 68,000. With the closure of Wembley for redevelopment, this meant that Old Trafford became the largest ground in the country. The new West Stand also included an area of the first tier that was set aside for families as well as more executive boxes.

Old Trafford hosted an all-Italian Champions League Final in May 2003 when

Milan and Juventus played out a goalless draw that was eventually settled by penalties. Two years later saw further expansion when the north-east and north-west quadrants of the ground gained a second tier each to add another 8,000 seats, leaving just the South Stand and its adjacent quadrants as the only single-tier structure in the ground. This provided Old Trafford with an increased capacity of 76,212 and a record attendance of 76,098 saw the home side beat Blackburn Rovers in March 2007 on their way to a 16th league title. The overall capacity of the ground was slightly reduced in 2009 as a result of seating reorganisation so any overhaul of that record will have to wait until the club can find a way of successfully redeveloping the South Stand.

◄ 1996

The easiest way to show Old Trafford's rapid expansion in the 21st century is to compare aerial views of the stadium as it hosted Euro 1996 with the size of the stadium as it looks today. In June 1996 crowds mill outside waiting to see the match between Russia and Germany with the massive North Stand towering over the rest of the ground. Over 50,000 saw Germany beat Russia 3-0 in the group stages with two goals from Jurgen Klinsmann.

▲ 2004

The stadium as it looked in the summer of 2004, now with large cantilevered stands at the Stretford (West) End and the East End, which once hosted the old scoreboard (see page 127). Significantly, much of the development occurred before the sale of the club in 2005. The quadrants linking the North Stand to the Stretford End and the East Stand have yet to be filled in.

▲ 2006

The 'Theatre of Dreams' with its major phases complete, photographed in December 2006. This aerial view makes it abundantly clear that the old South Stand, which houses the players' dressing rooms, is the one element not to scale with the rest of the ground. Fledgling plans have been put forward to build a new South Stand over the railway line and buy houses on the far side of the line, which would be dwarfed by the structure, but there are still many hurdles to overcome. The expansion would see the capacity rise to 95,000 – more than Wembley Stadium – and give Old Trafford the opportunity to host more England internationals to cater for fans living in the north of England. However, the height of the stand might also restrict the volume of light reaching the pitch, leading to the kind of playing surface problems experienced at the similarly towering Bernabéu in Madrid.

OLD TRAFFORD PILGRIMAGE

1974

The Manchester United Supporters' Club, Jersey branch, proudly show their colours in the Seventies. There are also branches on Guernsey, the Isle of Man and Gibraltar. The club's worldwide fan base includes more than 200 officially recognised branches of the MUSC in at least 24 countries, and United cater for this support through summer tours that take in the Far East, United States and all points in-between. It was estimated by the club in 2005 that United has 75 million fans worldwide – 23 million in Europe, 4.6 million in the Americas, 40.7 million in Asia and a further 5.9 million in South Africa.

A virtual-reality Old Trafford has been created in the Chinese city of Macau to allow supporters to enjoy the sensation of walking through the players' tunnel on to the pitch. They can also get a filmed dressing-room talk from Sir Alex Ferguson. As the average UK-based United supporter travels 2,234 miles a season following their idols, the 5,966 miles between the Macau 'Theatre of Dreams' and the real thing doubles this mileage on a one-way visit alone.

TODAY

A group of Asian fans arrive at Old Trafford in 2011. United have benefited from the Premier League's worldwide penetration. In 2009 English football was broadcast to 2.9 billion people in 212 different territories, with Asia the biggest regional market. The Reds' support is particularly strong in the East, with the 2005 signing of South Korean Park Ji-Sung one contributory factor. Hong Kong, Malaysia, Japan and Singapore each have their own dedicated fan club branches. They also have a Chinese-language website, on which Sir Alex Ferguson's comments are translated.

All this encourages visits to Old Trafford, and as Professor John Brooks of Manchester Metropolitan University says, 'Lots of foreign students first think of coming to Manchester (to study) because they support the team.'

But deep pockets are required; when six Asian billionaires pooled their funds and attempted to buy out the Glazers in 2009, it was said only two had recently visited Old Trafford to watch Sir Alex Ferguson and his players in Premier League action.

Manchester United Museum and Stadium Tour

To find out more about the unique history of Manchester United Football Club, you can visit the MUFC Museum at Old Trafford, as well as take an hour-long tour of the stadium. The museum is open seven days a week, but tours will not run on match days. Check opening times via the official website www.manutd.com

Further Reading

The Official Illustrated History of Manchester United 1878-2010: The Full Story and Complete Record (Simon and Schuster)

Manchester United: The Biography: The Complete Story of the World's Greatest Football Club by Jim White (Sphere)

Old Trafford: 100 Years at the Home of Manchester United: The Official Story by Ian Marshall (Simon and Schuster)

The Lost Babes: Manchester United and the Forgotten Victims of Munich by Jeff Connor (HarperSport)

When You Put on a Red Shirt: The Dreamers and their Dreams: Memories of Matt Busby, Jimmy Murphy and Manchester United by Keith Dewhurst (Yellow Jersey)

My Life in Football by Sir Bobby Charlton (Headline)

The King by Denis Law (Bantam)

Blessed – The Autobiography by George Best (Ebury)

Nobby Stiles: After the Ball – My Autobiography (Hodder and Stoughton)

Paddy Crerand: Never Turn the Other Cheek (HarperSport)

Determined: The Autobiography by Norman Whiteside (Headline)

The Doc's Devils: Manchester United 1972-1977 by Michael Crick (Cherry Red Books)

Manchester United – Man and Babe by Wilf McGuinness (Know the Score Books)

From Goal-Line to Touchline: My Career with Manchester United by Jack Crompton (Empire Publications)

Tooting Common to the Stretford End – The Alex Stepney Story by Alex Stepney and David Saffer (Vertical Editions)

Football, My Life by Lou Macari (Corgi)

Ryan Giggs: My Life, My Story (Headline)

Cantona: The Rebel Who Would Be King by Philippe Auclair (Pan)

INDEX

A

Albert Square 62, 118–19
Anderson, John 29
Arkesden, Tommy 16, 17
Armstrong, Joe 32, 33
Asian fans 140, 141
Aston, John 29, 116
Atkinson, Ron 90, 105
autograph hunters 78–9
Aytoun Street 60–1

B

Bacon, Fred 18, 19
Bacon, Jack 16, 17
Bank Street 10, 12–13, 23
Bannister, Jimmy 17, 18, 19
Beckham, David 77, 93, 99, 100, 108, 129
Beddow, John 16, 17
Bell, Alex 16, 17, 18, 19
Bent, Geoff 38
Berbatov, Dimitar 79
Bergkamp, Dennis 93
Berry, Johnny 31, 36, 38, 57, 58
Best, George 15, 49, 65, 78, 79, 80–9, 96–7, 102–3, 106, 110, 115, 116, 131
Bishop, Bob 80
Black, Sam 8
Blackburn Olympic 6
Blackstock, Tommy 16, 17
Blanchflower, Jackie 29, 31, 32, 33, 38, 41
Bloom Street 15
Bonthron, Bob 16, 17
Brennan, June 68
Brennan, Shay 46, 64, 65
Bridge Street 89
Bridgewater Canal 25
Brooks, John 141
Broomfield, Herbert 18
Broughton Rangers 108
Burgess, Herbert 17, 18
'Busby Babes' 31, 35, 51
Busby, Jean 39, 42, 50
Busby, Sir Matt 26, 27, 28, 29, 31, 33, 34, 38, 39, 42, 43, 47, 48–55, 56, 67, 73, 75, 80, 81, 82, 86, 92, 96, 97, 101, 106, 110, 115, 116, 117
Busby, Sandy 42, 106
Byrne, Roger 31, 35, 38, 91

C

Cantona, Eric 9, 93, 105, 131
Cantwell, Noel 115
Carey, Johnny 29
Carrick, Michael 68
Carrick, Lisa 68
Carrick, Michael 85
Carrington 108, 109, 112–13
Carrington Moss 112
cars 100–5
Central Park 7
Champions League 55, 57, 77, 119, 138
Charlton, Bobby 31, 32, 33, 35, 37, 38, 39, 41, 45, 49, 50, 56, 59, 64, 65, 66, 67, 68, 70–5, 93, 96–7, 101, 106, 108, 110, 115, 116, 117, 118, 133
Charlton, Elizabeth 70
Charlton, Gordon 70

Charlton, Jackie 70
Charlton, Tommy 70
Charlton, Norma 68, 72
Charlton, Suzanne 72
Chester Road 98, 99
Clayton, Gordon 32, 33
Cliff training ground 106, 108–9, 100–11, 112–13
Colman, Eddie 32, 33, 35, 38, 58
Connelly, John 78
Crane, Frazer 89
Crerand, Pat 67, 90, 106, 100, 115, 131
Crickmer, Walter 41, 57, 76
Crompton, Jack 59, 106
Cross Street, Sale 89
Crowther, Stan 46
Curry, Tom 41

D

Daly, Gerry 135
Davies, Elsie 14
Davies, John Henry 14, 17, 26, 124
Delaney, Jimmy 31
Docherty, Tommy 49, 90, 94, 110
Donaldson, Bob 10
Doughty, Jack 8
Downie, Alex 16, 17, 18
Downie, John 31
Doughty, Roger 8
Duckworth, Dick 18, 19, 133
Dunne, Ann 68
Dunne, Pat 131
Dunne, Tony 91, 110, 131

E

East Stand 55, 121, 123, 127, 129, 131, 138, 139
Edwardia 89
Edwards, Duncan 29, 31, 32, 33, 35, 38, 39, 44–5, 79, 93, 108
Eriksson, Sven-Goran 111
European Cup 31, 34, 53, 55, 56–7, 81, 82, 94, 116–17

F

FA Charity Shield 17
FA Cup 18–19, 20, 23, 28–9, 31, 46–7, 49, 53, 114–15, 119
Fardon, Don 89
Ferdinand, Rio 85, 105
Ferguson, Sir Alex 9, 41, 51, 52, 53, 54, 67, 95, 97, 99, 105, 107, 109, 113, 133, 140, 141
Ferry, Noreen 68
Fitzpatrick, John 80
Fitzpatrick, Tony 74
Foulkes, Bill 35, 38, 46, 58, 64, 65, 73, 117
Fullaway, Mrs 80, 85

G

G-Mex 21
Gaskell, Dave 115
Gibson, James W. 26, 29, 76, 108, 125
Giggs, Ryan 70, 99, 100, 105, 108
Gill, David 41
Gillies, Matt 115
Glazer family 77
Goodman, Pearl 86
Great Stone Road 65

Greater Manchester Exhibition and Conference Centre 21
Gregg, Harry 35, 38, 41, 46, 47, 50

H

Halse, Harold 18, 19
Haraldsted, Eva 103
Hardaker, Alan 56
Hayes, Vince 18
Haynes, Johnny 86
Healey, William 14
Hederbyl, Siv 103
Herd, David 91, 101, 115
Herd, Joan 68
Herberger, Sepp 39
Hillsborough disaster 135, 137
Holden, Dick 18, 19
Huber, Hans 39
Hughes, Mark 104–5
Hughes, Mark 9

I

Imperial Hotel 14–15

J

Jaaks, Sigrid 39
Jackson, Philip 55
Ji-Sung, Park 113, 141
Jones, Mark 32, 33, 35, 38, 39, 58

K

K Stand 129
Kickz 111
Kidd, Brian 65, 106, 116, 117

L

Lancashire & Yorkshire Railway 7
Law, Denis 49, 58, 59, 67, 73, 86, 91, 92–7, 100, 101, 106, 115, 131, 134
Law, Diana 68
Lawton, James 117
Leitch, Archibald 133
Lowry art gallery 87
Lukic, Vesna 41

M

Macari, Lou 90, 91, 135
Macau 140
Maierboeck, Ludwig 39
Main Stand 25, 27, 42, 124, 125, 131
Maine Road 25, 27, 28
Malmaison Hotel 15
Manchester Central Station 20–1
Manchester City 26
Manchester Ship Canal 87, 124
Manchester United Junior Athletic Club 29, 108
Manchester United-ettes 69
Manchester Velodrome 13
Manchesterplatz memorial 41
Mangnall, Ernest 16, 17, 18, 19, 23, 133
Martins, Daniela 69
McGoldrick, Rita 99
McGuinness, Wilf 54, 58, 66, 67, 75, 91, 106, 110, 117
McIlroy, Sammy 134
McNarry, Barbara 97
Mears, Joe 75
Meredith, Billy 17, 18, 19, 133
Midland Hotel 66–7

Mitten, Charlie 29, 31
Moger, Harry 16, 17, 18, 19
Mollard, Valerie 39
Mooney, Malcolm 86, 87
Morgans, Kenny 35, 38
Moston Brook High School 11
MUFA Megastore 123
Muhrer, Georgs 50
Munich air crash 34, 36–42
Munich Clock 43
Munich plaque 42
Murphy, Jimmy 28, 29, 32, 33, 39, 46, 47, 50, 73, 92, 106
Musgrove, Malcolm 110

N

Nani, Luis 69, 105
Neville, Gary 108
Newton Heath 10, 11, 12
Newton Heath Carriage and Wagon works 7
Newton Heath Engineering Works 6–7
Newton Heath L&YR 6, 8–9
Nicholson, Jimmy 64, 65
Norbreck Hydro 106
North Manchester Business Park 7, 11
North Road 10–11
North Stand 127, 131, 137, 139
Northampton Road 11
Nuttall, J. 18

O

O'Farrell, Frank 110, 131
Old Trafford 22–5, 26–7, 28–9, 124–39
Old Trafford cricket ground 63
Olive, Les 92
Oscars nightclub 89

P

Parker, Paul 9
Pearson, Stan 29, 31
Pearson, Stuart 135
Peddie, Jack 16, 17
Pegg, David 33, 38, 66, 67
Peronace, Gigi 92
Piccadilly Gardens 60, 61
Piccadilly Station 46, 47, 58, 61
Picken, Jack 16, 17, 18, 19
Plaza Ballroom 33
Popular Side 124, 127
Powell, Jack 8

Q

Queiroz, Carlos 107
Quicks showroom 98–9
Quixall, Jeanette 68, 115

R

Railway Road 30–1
Red Devils Souvenir Shop 122–3
Red Star Belgrade 34, 35
Rhodes, Alan 32, 33
Rimmer, Jimmy 117
Roberts, Charlie 14, 16, 17, 18, 19, 20
Ronaldo, Cristiano 93, 105
Rooney, Wayne 55, 59, 105, 107
Rowley, Jack 29
Rocca, Louis 14

S

Sadler, David 73, 80, 81, 91, 101, 106
Sagar, Charles 16, 17
Salford Quays 87
Savile, Jimmy 33
Scanlon, Albert 35, 38
Scholes, Paul 108
Scoreboard End 127, 129, 131
Setters, Pat 68
Sharp, Lee 9
Sir Matt Busby Way 55, 63, 121, 125
Slack Alice nightclub 15, 89
Small Heath 8
South Stand 25, 121, 125, 133, 138
Stacey, George 18
Stafford, Harry 14, 18
Stanley, Ken 86, 87
Stepney, Alex 67, 110
Stiles, Nobby 59, 100, 117, 118, 127, 133
Stretford End 27, 127, 135, 137, 139
Summerbee, Mike 89
supporters 76–7
supporter's clubs 140–1
Swift, Frank 41

T

Taylor, Ernie 46
Taylor, J. 18
Taylor, Tommy 31, 33, 35, 38, 57, 66, 67
Tevz, Carlos 95
Thane, Captain 41
Trafford Park 23
Trafford Training Centre 109, 112–13
train travel 58–9
training 106–7
Travis, Dave Lee 33
Turnbull, Jimmy 18, 19
Turnbull, Sandy 17, 18, 19

U

United Road Stand 127, 131
Urbini, Max 83
van der Sar, Edwin 105

V

Viollet, Dennis 29, 31, 35, 38, 41, 57

W

Wall, George 17, 18, 19
Warwick Road 62–3, 120–1
Watson, Mrs 32, 33, 51
Webster, Colin 50
West Stand 137, 138, 139
Whalley, Bert 32, 33, 41
Whelan, Billy 66, 67
Whelan, Liam 31, 32, 33, 38
White, Bill 86
wives and girlfriends (WAGS) 68–9
Wood, Ray 31, 38
World War II 25, 26–7